PRAISE FOR

—The Beginn
Heari

James Goll moves in a high real............tion but writes in a very down-to-earth and practical way about hearing God's voice. This foundational book will change your life.

Dr. Ché Ahn
Author, *How to Pray for Healing* and *Hosting the Holy Spirit*
Senior Pastor, Harvest Rock Church
Pasadena, California

James Goll has lived many years of hearing God's voice. All of us have much we can learn from him.

John Arnott
Senior Pastor, Toronto Airport Christian Fellowship
Toronto, Ontario, Canada

This transparent personal presentation goes way beyond being a beginner's guide—it is a hands-on spiritual guidance manual chock full of principles distilled from decades of daily practice. Most important, this balanced study outlines scriptural and practical steps to test divine guidance. Every openhearted follower of Jesus of Nazareth will be enriched and propelled forward into more effective Kingdom-bringing by this excellent study!

Gary Bergel
President, Intercessors for America and Youth Interceding for America

Some years ago, when we were looking for a prophetic voice to bring to the Belmont Church to help us learn to listen for God, we called James Goll. We were not disappointed with his easy-to-apply guidelines for following hard after the voice of God. *The Beginner's Guide to Hearing God* is exactly what the title indicates—an easy-to-read, easy-to-apply beginner's guide to listening to God and discerning how God is speaking to you. I find that it also has good reminders for those of us who have been listening for a while.

Don Finto
Author, *Your People Shall Be My People*

One of the most exciting occurrences in a believer's life is hearing the voice of God for the very first time. What an empowering and memorable experience! In his profound work, *The Beginner's Guide to Hearing God*, James Goll assures the reader that God can and will speak personally to him or her. His excellently shared principles and easy-to-relate-to illustrations will incite a greater desire within you to hear the Father's voice. This book is a must-read for those who are seeking to know the heart of God, because the first step to knowing His heart is hearing His voice!

Dr. Kingsley A. Fletcher
International Speaker, Government Adviser, Author and Pastor
Research Triangle Park, North Carolina

After observing James Goll in ministry, it would be extremely easy to conclude that he has reached an unattainable dimension of clarity in hearing from God, and that he is a one-of-a-kind modern-day Elijah. James decided not to let the Body of Christ off the hook so easily. This book has been written with every believer in mind. It demystifies the process of hearing from God and invites the reader into a deeper relationship with the Lord. *The Beginner's Guide to Hearing God* covers theological and devotional approaches to hearing from God in a disarmingly simple but profound perspective. I literally wept as I read the last chapter of this book. It impacted me that much! Get ready for a life-changing experience.

Harry R. Jackson, Jr.
Senior Pastor, Hope Christian Church
Washington, D.C.

James Goll guides the reader through the pitfalls and the mountaintops of hearing God's voice—a gift the enemy hates so much. Only a seasoned prophetic voice like James's could write with such wisdom, passion and insight. Following the guidelines covered within these pages almost guarantees opening the readers' ears to hear anything God might be saying.

John Paul Jackson
Founder and Chair, Streams Ministries International

If you have ever longed to hear God in a clearer way, *The Beginner's Guide to Hearing God* is for you. James Goll has long had an intimate relationship with God and knows how to communicate well what God has taught him. This book guides you in practical and biblical ways in learning how to listen more closely. If you are willing, you can move from a hard-to-receive (HTR) position to one he calls ETR—easy-to-receive. Fresh insights he shares from recent experiences will make us desire to listen more closely for the voice of the Holy Spirit with attentive and expectant hearts. Thanks, James, for another great book!

Quin Sherrer
Coauthor, *The Beginner's Guide to Receiving the Holy Spirit*

— The — Beginner's Guide to

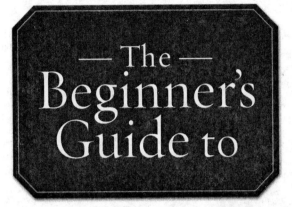

Hearing God

JAMES W. GOLL

Regal

From Gospel Light
Ventura, California, U.S.A.

Published by Regal
From Gospel Light
Ventura, California, U.S.A.
www.regalbooks.com
Printed in the U.S.A.

All Scripture quotations, unless otherwise indicated, are taken from the *New American Standard Bible,* © 1960, 1962, 1963, 1968, 1971, 1972, 1973, 1975, 1977 by The Lockman Foundation. Used by permission.

Other versions used are
KJV—King James Version. Authorized King James Version.
NKJV—Scripture taken from the *New King James Version.* Copyright © 1979, 1980, 1982 by Thomas Nelson, Inc. Used by permission. All rights reserved.
NLT—Scripture quotations marked *NLT* are taken from the *Holy Bible,* New Living Translation, copyright © 1996. Used by permission of Tyndale House Publishers, Inc., Wheaton, Illinois 60189. All rights reserved.

© 2004, 2008 James Goll
All rights reserved.

Library of Congress Cataloging-in-Publication Data
Goll, James W.
  The beginner's guide to hearing God / James W. Goll
     p. cm.
  Includes bibliographical references.
  ISBN 978-08307-4611-8
1. Discernment of spirits. 2. Christian life. I. Title.
  BV5083.G65 2004
  248.4—dc22

                                                        2003027466

Rights for publishing this book outside the U.S.A. or in non-English languages are administered by Gospel Light Worldwide, an international not-for-profit ministry. For additional information, please visit www.glww.org, email info@glww.org, or write to Gospel Light Worldwide, 1957 Eastman Avenue, Ventura, CA 93003, U.S.A.

With an overflowing heart of thanksgiving,
I wish to dedicate this book to two of my mentors in
hearing God's voice. The Holy Spirit brought these two
gifted men into my life, and they have made a dramatic
impact on my destiny. Years ago, Mahesh Chavda
taught me some of his best-kept secrets about hearing
God. May the Lord reward you, Mahesh. I am also
indebted to my "prophetic papa," Bob Jones, who took
me under his wing in the early years of
the prophetic movement.

Contents

Acknowledgments

Deep gratitude goes to my staff and team at Encounters Network (formerly Ministry to the Nations) for its support in every project I undertake. The Prayer Shield relentlessly intercedes for me, for which I am thankful. I am everlastingly grateful to my dear family, always standing by my side. I need you, oh, I need you!

I also wish to thank my friend Quin Sherrer, who opened the door for the publishing of this manuscript. Finally, I want to thank my editor for this project, Kathy Deering, and the great staff and team at Regal Books.

The Beginner's Guide series has done a great job in filling a real need in the Body of Christ. I am honored to contribute to this series and trust that everyone who reads *The Beginner's Guide to Hearing God* will fall in love with the Master's voice.

Chapter One

Our Need to Hear God

My sheep hear My voice, and I know them, and they follow Me.
JOHN 10:27

*Behold, I stand at the door and knock; if anyone hears
My voice and opens the door, I will come in to him,
and will dine with him, and he with Me.*
REVELATION 3:20

Does God really speak today? Will He speak personally
to me? If I listen, will He speak in such a manner that
even *I* can understand? Thank God, the answer is yes!
And, believe it or not (I expect you will believe it by the
time you finish this book), God Himself wants all of us
to hear what He is saying—more than any of us do!

Each of us was created with a deep inner longing to
hear our Master's voice. He didn't make us to be mech-
anical robots that just march around doing preordained
things. Our Father God created us to have fellowship with
Him. It is our birthright to have an actual relationship
with our God.

If our yearning for an intimate relationship with
the lover of our souls is to be fulfilled, hearing His voice
is a must. We cannot grow in our relationship with God

unless we draw near to Him, trusting that He wants to speak to us personally.

Jesus came to restore humankind into the sweet fellowship that Adam and Eve first had known in the Garden. Sin cut them off from God and they could no longer be close to God. Sin in the same way today cuts off each of us from God. But sin doesn't have the final word. Because of the cross and the shed blood of Christ Jesus, we can be restored to fellowship. One of the main reasons Jesus came was to enable us to walk in restored communion with God.

From my perspective, the greatest need in the Church today is for believers to clearly hear the voice of God for themselves. For us to reach our potential for an intimate relationship with God, we must be able to communicate with Him. Communication with God goes two ways: (1) talking to Him and (2) listening to Him when He talks to us. To have good communication, we must learn how and when to speak up and how to push the "pause button" in order to listen.

Most of us seem to do okay on the first one. But we have to take the time to learn the lost art of listening to Him, expectantly.

It Takes Two

Fellowship is not a one-way road. It takes at least two, with both parties—in one another's presence—sharing attentively in some kind of communion. Our relationship with our heavenly Papa was never meant to be a long-distance telephone conversation.

"Available" is God's middle name. He is just aching to spend time alone with each of us. He yearns to hear from us. He wants us to know how attentive He is.

As I travel in my ministry, I am often away from my family for days at a time, but I diligently attempt to keep in touch with what is happening at home. Some times I do a better job than at others. Using today's wonderful modern technology—cell phones, faxes, email and such—my wife and I attempt to keep in touch. But cell phone calls and email messages do not compare or replace being with my dear wife and family. Sometimes I just need a hug! True love requires being together. The greatest key to hearing God's voice is cultivating a love-based relationship.

Mark Virkler states it this way: "The voice of God, I've discovered, is Spirit-to-spirit communication, the Holy Spirit speaking directly to my spirit."[1] True fellowship requires that both parties speak and listen, both sharing their hearts deeply with one another. This is the key to keeping all relationships fresh and alive. In an atmosphere of trust, we share our heart with someone else. Communion with God is much more than a ritual or an "information time." It's Spirit-to-spirit time!

Dutch Sheets said, "What topic could possibly deserve more of our attention than listening to God? When the source of all life and wisdom speaks, those who would be wise listen. The foolish either don't care to or don't learn how. The fruit of both is the same: destructive ignorance."[2] We do not want to walk in the path of destruction but in the path of life. Oh God, deliver us from formulaic Christianity and restore to us the pathways of constant dependency. Teach us the ways of life. Teach us to live transparent, shared lives.

As for me, I want to hear His voice and intimately know Him, not just on a casual basis, but also on a daily, vibrant one. Join me and thousands of others who are learning to hear the Master's beckoning voice by leaning our ear toward Him. Come with me now on a journey of beginning to hear (and love hearing) God's voice.

How It Began with Me

By the grace of God and the influence of my praying mother and church community, I grew up knowing that Jesus was my best friend. As a child, I would go on long walks in rural Missouri and just talk incessantly to God. Often, while gazing into the skies, I would try to listen to see if He had anything to say back.

As the youngest child, with two older sisters, I always had wanted a brother. So Jesus became the brother I never had. Years passed, and I graduated from high school. But one thing remained the same—Jesus was right there with me as my close friend.

At college, I hungered for more of God. This quest led me into divine collision with a group of people with whom this straight-laced, rural Methodist kid did not have much in common—the Jesus People. When I got filled with the Holy Spirit and released into His gifts in the Jesus Movement, it was like my little black-and-white TV set turned into OmniVision overnight. I was absolutely transformed.

Suddenly, my life was very different. I had attempted to walk with the Lord all along, but now my life in the

Spirit took a quantum leap. Somehow I had been able to detect His voice before, but in comparison to what I had previously experienced, now it was as if God had just given me a hearing aid. I really didn't know what to do with all this stuff—impressions, mental snapshots, hunches, knowledge, short thoughts and full phrases that were being released into my heart and mind. But the Holy Spirit became an awesome tutor to me on this immense learning curve.

Still being quite young in this realm, I thought all believers lived this way. I thought that at last I was living the "normal Christian life." (And I still think it is supposed to be that way!) I didn't realize how many believers cannot point to one single instance of hearing God's voice for themselves. Yet even with my heightened experience of God, I knew I needed more if I was to really advance in maturity in hearing and knowing His voice.

A Desire for Discernment

In the middle of my junior year at Central Missouri State University, this drive to know God led me to cry out for discernment. Late one night, I went to pray with another Jesus freak in an Episcopal church where a friend's father, an evangelical, Spirit-filled Episcopal priest, was the rector. At the front of the sanctuary, on the wall close to the Communion rail, there was a lighted candle. It was a symbolic representation of the light of God and presence of God. I loved sneaking away when I could to spend time in quiet reflection, as His sweet presence seemed to reside there.

While basking in the light of His presence late that same night, I began to vocalize my desire to hear and know the voice of God better. I proceeded logically:

Based on John 10:27, You have stated, "My sheep hear My voice, and I know them and they follow Me." Now I don't have any problem with the first part of the verse, "My sheep hear My voice." I know I have heard Your voice because in Revelation 3:20 it says, "Behold, I stand at the door and knock; if anyone hears My voice and opens the door, I will come in to him, and will dine with him, and he with Me." I have heard Your knock at the door of my heart and I am one of Yours.

I continued with my line-by-line presentation:

So, Father, I accept by faith that I do hear Your voice. The second part of the verse I don't have any problem with either. I know that You know me, and You know me better than I know myself. I don't have any problem with that. But it's the third part of that verse that I have a big problem with, "and they follow Me." So, God, I need to do more than just hear Your voice—because I also hear my voice, the voice of my flesh, the voice of others, the voice of the world and the voice of the enemy, Satan. Therefore, if I'm going to be able to "follow You," I must do more than only hear Your voice. I need to be able to discern Your voice from the other voices.

That night, my friend and I knelt in prayer and simply said, "Lord, we ask that You enroll us in Your School of the Spirit. Teach us not only how to hear but also how to discern Your voice from the voice of the stranger and all the other voices that contend for our attention. Please do this so that we can truly follow You."

Perhaps there is a book in heaven called *The Book of Godly Desires* that God keeps a record in. All I know is that night in November 1972, it seemed to me that the Lord wrote down my name in His book. I enrolled in His School of the Spirit. Thirty-plus years later, I'm still taking various classes in that school. I don't think I've graduated from it yet. I want to be among those who are continuously learning how to hear and discern His wonderful voice and how to follow Him.

How about you?

Lessons from the Original Couple

A good starting place in this School of the Spirit is the lessons we can learn from the original couple, Adam and Eve, as recorded in Genesis 3. After they tasted the forbidden fruit, God came looking for some fellowship with Adam and Eve—to walk and talk with them (as He does with you and me). In *The Coming Prophetic Revolution*, I wrote about what this must have been like:

> Can you imagine, after Adam and Eve had known God, and He knew them, how quickly the spiritual climate changed? As a result of their disobedience, they experienced instantaneous barriers to their intimacy with Him. Walls shot up. After

their sin they plucked off leaves from the nearest bush as quickly as they could and sewed coverings for themselves. They were hiding from the Lord their Creator for the first time in their lives.

But God, in His passionate pursuit, was still drawing close. A new reaction stirred within them as He drew near. Previously they had run toward the sound of His footsteps. Now they ran in the opposite direction. Before, their response had been for joy: "Oh, wow, it's Father!" Now it was dread and fear: "Oh, no, it's Father!" They were guilt-ridden. Never had they had such an emotional reaction or even such a thought before! They had not known condemnation or fear or shame. Now, as a result of their disobedience, they ran and hid from the voice of God.[3]

This pretty well sums up the difference between the joy of hearing God and obeying His voice and the dilemma of hearing God's voice and *not* obeying.

Here's the good news: God is searching for us. He is drawing near—whether we want Him to or not! He is the glorious intruder. God does not give up on His beloved; He wants to walk and talk with you. But there can be some sad news also—barriers to intimacy result when we choose to ignore what He tells us. So let's listen up and learn. We need Him. We need to hear His voice. Let's cultivate a heart and life that responds when He speaks.

From the Pioneer of Faith

Many pilgrims of the faith have walked this path before us. We can look to them and learn from both their failures and their successes. They needed to hear God in their day just as we do in ours. And God drew near to them in His loving grace just as He will draw near to us.

With this in mind, let's look at the life of Abraham, who is called the father and pioneer of our faith. This man heard impossible promises from God, things that would require God's presence for their fulfillment. (By the way, a good test of whether we have heard God is that He rarely asks us to do something that we can do in our own strength or by our own effort. God doesn't want to give us a mere word—He wants to create a constant need in us for more of Him!)

Abraham had to feel rather desperate and dependent, don't you think? God required everything of Abraham. Through miraculous intervention, the promised son finally was born—in Abraham's old age. But when this precious son, Isaac, reached early manhood, God spoke to Abraham again and told him to take his son and offer him as a sacrifice on Mount Moriah (see Gen. 22:1-2). What a test! But Abraham obeyed, and what an outcome! At the zero hour, God supplied a ram that could be sacrificed in place of Isaac, and God was satisfied. This makes Abraham our finest example of believing God and obeying Him fully.

Have you ever had to learn the grace of yielding? Have you ever wanted to hold on too tightly to every little bit you have? I know I have. But as I see more of the revelation of His great love for me, I, like Abraham, eventually melt and yield to His kingdom ways. So will you as you too learn to walk this pilgrimage of faith.

Abraham was called the "friend" of God (see 2 Chron. 20:7). How did he become God's friend? Maybe it was because he was with Him so much. He became familiar with God's voice, and he learned to recognize even His shadow when He was walking past.

I too want to be the friend of God. In fact, that is what I think hearing God's voice is all about.

We Each Have a Desperate Need

Many other people in the Bible are examples for us of how to maintain a personal relationship with God. As distinctly different as they are in personality and circumstances, they all show us a desperate face. Oh, to be like Moses, who talked to God face to face. But please, Lord, save me from 40 years of wilderness wandering! If we want to hear God in the gentle breeze as Elijah did, then we must be aware that it might involve getting the moody blues and hiding out in a cave. If we want angelic encounters like Daniel had, then we must get ready for the fire of God's furnace as well!

If we want to do the impossible, we must simply respond as a young teenaged girl named Mary responded when she received the words of an angel and conceived a gift from God. (*But, God, that was a one-time deal, right?*) Or simply be like Paul, the amazing apostle, who recognized that the words he heard from the Lord were to prepare him for the costs that lay ahead.

There are scores of others, of course. They may seem famous to us now, but Abraham, Moses, Mary and Paul were only ordinary people like us. Each person ever created has a need and a longing to hear our Creator's voice. Each person can talk to God, and we can hear Him, too.

Each person is created with the need to be continuously dependent on His voice. I think of the words of an old hymn: "I need Thee, O I need Thee; Every hour I need Thee."

We all need to hear and know the voice of our Father, the voice of the Son, Jesus, and that of the Holy Spirit, our Helper, Guide and Comforter. All three desire to speak to us. It's all about being in God's presence.

Veteran teacher and author Fuchsia Pickett states:

> We must enter into unity with God's will for our lives through divine revelation. Christ wants our minds to think His thoughts and our wills to choose His will to be performed in and through us. [This happens as] we cultivate our relationship with Christ.[4]

Perhaps you too will add your name to the list of those who heard God speak and then became strong in faith, doing mighty exploits in His great name. Remember, "faith comes by hearing" (Rom. 10:17, *NKJV*). Take time to listen for His voice with all your heart. Are you ready to get started in a few lessons?

Enroll Now!

You don't have to wait any longer—classes start every day! School is in session at all times! You can enroll right now and be a student with me in the School of the Spirit, where we learn to hear the voice of God. If this echoes the cry of your heart, pray:

> *Dear Lord, I want to hear Your voice and learn Your ways. Be my Teacher and Guide. Enroll me in the*

School of the Spirit and teach me to hear Your voice.
Write down my name! I want to know You, be a disciple
of Christ Jesus, and have sweet communion with You.
I want to hear You, I want to have more faith, and
I want to obey what You tell me. Help, Lord,
Your servant wants to listen! Amen.

Think About It

1. If we are satisfied and contented with the status quo of our spiritual lives, we will never try very hard to hear God's voice. But when we're desperate for guidance or for reassurance, we'll hasten to consult Him. On a scale of 1 to 10, how desperate are you to hear God's voice? The 1 represents complete satisfaction with your present life and 10 means you feel trapped and stuck and that you'd do just about anything to be able to hear from Him.

    1   2   3   4   5   6   7   8   9   10

2. Have you ever heard God's voice? What did it sound like? Were you aware at first that it was the voice of God?

Chapter Two

Our Personal Tutor

But I tell you the truth, it is to your advantage that I go away;
for if I do not go away, the Helper shall not come to you;
but if I go, I will send Him to you.

JOHN 16:7

However, when He, the Spirit of truth, has come,
He will guide you into all truth; for He will not speak on
His own authority, but whatever He hears He will speak;
and He will tell you things to come.

JOHN 16:13, *NKJV*

When the Helper comes, whom I will send to you
from the Father, that is the Spirit of truth, who proceeds
from the Father, He will bear witness of Me.

JOHN 15:26

Our Papa God has many gifts to give to us. The biggest gift of all, of course, is His Son, Jesus—yes, Jesus, the beloved Son, who through the work of the cross purchased for us our salvation, redemption, atonement from our sins and eternal life and promised to be our Bridegroom that great day in the future. Our heavenly Father gave us His very heart in that One Gift. He is the greatest gift of all.

Jesus, in turn, gives us wonderful gifts of His love: promises He will keep, cleansing, hope, healing, deliverance, hugs, kisses, and lots of other good things—all of which come from the heart of His Father. The gift of Jesus' shed blood alone, with all the power and love that it carries, is beyond our understanding.

Father and Son have sent their best to us by giving each of us disciples one very special gift, a gift that keeps giving us more gifts. What could that be? It's our Comforter, our Guide, the One called alongside to help us out—the Holy Spirit. The Holy Spirit allows us to sense our Father God's personal loving touch. Getting to know what His touch feels like is a lifelong adventure.

Getting to Know the Third Person of the Godhead

Although I loved and accepted Christ as my personal Savior at a very young age, for many years the Holy Spirit was just a ghost to me. That's what the Apostles' Creed that I recited in church every Sunday stated so simply: "I believe in the Holy Ghost." I don't remember much else being taught about this third Person of the Godhead in the rural Protestant church where I was reared. I knew that He wasn't Casper the Friendly Ghost, but I wasn't quite sure who He really was or what He came to do. Jesus I knew as my friend; I was getting used to God as my Father. But who was this Holy Ghost?

It all remained a bit of a mystery—until I ran into some wild Jesus fanatics! They sang strange songs, such as the "Holy Ghost Will Set Your Feet A-Dancin'"! (Huh?

He will do *what*? With *whom*? Not me, dude!) As time went on, I fell even more in love with Jesus and also grew fanatical about the things of the Holy Spirit. He quickly became one of my closest companions.

Today, He indeed is my friend, partner, guide and co-conspirator. He wants to be yours as well. But to get close to Him, you may have to push through misconceptions, spiritual warfare, debates about religious theories and a bunch of just plain old opposition, until you come to the place where you and He are rightly related with one another and on good speaking terms.

My friend Quin Sherrer and her coauthor Ruthanne Garlock wrote:

> What an extraordinary gift the Father bestowed upon his children when he sent the Holy Spirit to be our helper! Is it any wonder that Satan tries to minimize the significance of the gift and divide and confuse the body of Christ concerning it?[1]

Veteran pastor David Wilkerson, founder of Teen Challenge, adds the following timeless insight:

> Give much quality time to communion with the Holy Spirit. He will not speak to anyone who is in a hurry. All of God's word is about waiting on Him! . . . Wait patiently. Seek the Lord and minister praises to Him. Take authority over every other voice that whispers thoughts to you. Believe that the Spirit is greater than these are, and that He will not let you be deceived or blind. Be willing to set your heart on Him.[2]

Many Christians know a lot about the Holy Spirit. They write great detailed books and go into the Greek lexicon to explain Him. They quote the Old Testament and the New Testament. Some can instruct us by descriptively defining all of His diverse functions. All of this is valuable.

But in the midst of all of it, stop and ask yourself, *Do I really, really know the Holy Spirit as a person, as someone with whom I am becoming intimate? Is He really my friend, my Helper, my Comforter and my Guide?* Even if you feel you cannot honestly say that you know the Holy Spirit yet, remember that a love relationship is a two-way street. He is right beside you, waiting to be entreated. He is waiting to be engaged.

The Tutor of God's Personal Touch

The Holy Spirit is our counselor and our teacher, yet He is more than a teacher—more like a tutor. But He is not just any tutor; He's the kind who truly loves to spend individual, personal time with each of His students. He is like that rare kind of guidance counselor who actually becomes a friend. He is like the teacher who becomes a personal mentor.

As a good teacher, I respect the Spirit highly. But as my personal tutor, I have such warm affection for Him. I never had that for any other teacher or, in some ways, any earthly friend.

To help us gain a little more light on the subject, let's glance at how the term "tutor" is described in the dictionary.

tutor *n*: a person charged with the instruction and guidance of another as a private teacher

tutor *vi* 1: to have guardianship, tutelage, or care of 2: to teach or guide usually individually in a special subject or for a particular purpose : COACH ˜ *vi* 1: to do the work of a tutor 2: to receive instruction especially privately[3]

Here we see more of the potential for the special kind of relationship we can have with the Holy Spirit. As a personal Tutor, He is also a personal coach to help us win out on the playing field of life.

In addition—great news!—He's not like an ordinary tutor or teacher who clocks in and out. As we graduate from one level of spiritual development to the next, He remains our lifelong personal Tutor. We start with the best and we end with the best. As we end our days here on Earth, He even prepares us for our postgraduate course in life hereafter! All along, He individually instructs us as to what life lessons we need to learn, and even in what order to take them.

Who Has Influenced Your Life?

When asked the question, What one person in your life has influenced you the most? often people answer with the name of a special schoolteacher or coach they had when growing up. I know what my answer would be: Besides Jesus Himself, the Holy Spirit has made more of an impact on my life than any person has.

The Holy Spirit leaves an immeasurable impact upon our lives. He is able to teach, influence and comfort—all at the same time, always with the most careful love. Jesus loves us, this we know, but the Holy Spirit shows us that

God even *likes* us! God, in the person of the Holy Spirit, likes hanging out with us, and we with Him.

The quality of the time we spend fellowshipping with the Holy Spirit has everything to do with hearing God's voice. I love to ask Him questions. My mother always said I was a very curious child. With God we all can be curious cats. Go ahead, ask Him questions. The more specific we become in our asking, the more detailed His answers to us will be.

In fact, pause right now and ask God a question. He will answer! Watch out, though, the Holy Spirit might turn around and ask *you* some questions, perhaps even give you some tests to take.

Many Classes to Take

God offers such a variety of tremendous classes in His School of the Spirit. This Tutor specializes in teaching subjects that are not the same as the ones we find in worldly institutions, because He has something more in mind than merely imparting knowledge. He tutors to transform lives! He offers classes such as Holiness 101, which, of course, is followed by the Fire of Holiness 102. Then, after we get a fresh grip on holiness (or it does on us!), we jump up into Victorious Living 201. Maybe eventually we will graduate into upper-level classes such as Humility 301 and Death to Self 302.

In a different department of His school, we consider His revelatory teaching grace. With Him at our elbow, we learn to dissect the Word of God instead of frogs. Instead of learning how to diagram sentences or describe verbs and their tenses, He introduces us to the Author of the Word of God, launching us on an eternity-spanning exploration.

One of His tutorial specialties is one of my favorites: a class on foreign languages (the gift of speaking in tongues). Admittance is open to anyone who has taken the prerequisite class, Salvation 101. After that, there is another related course called Interpretation of Tongues 102. Our Guide will enable us to pray in a language we don't have to study in the traditional way, with ongoing help to translate what we have prayed.

So it goes. By the way, all of these lessons hone our study skills—we will get better and better at hearing the voice of God. (Our personal Tutor is quite interested in that part.)

By the way, history classes are a very important area of expertise for the Holy Spirit. His slant on history is one that is entirely accurate. It is not biased nor does it favor any one certain economic group, nationality or political view. All of life is actually His story.

He teaches us how we fit into the big picture; He builds our personal history with God. While meeting our needs for the present moment, He establishes something permanent in us for the future, His unshakeable kingdom. Thus we are prepared for the real world, the eternal world, where things that really matter include faith, hope, compassion and, above all, true love. We learn that holiness, righteousness and honesty are far more important than how to read the stock market and that sacrificial giving is foundational if we want our life story to show that we have followed in Jesus' footsteps.

The School of the Future

We find another area of study in God's School of the Future. Can you imagine a real class in which the teacher actually knows the future, a professor who can teach history before it happens? The Holy Spirit knows it all. He even knows everything about you! He is omniscient. He sometimes releases preview clips of things to come. As a part of His job description as our personal coach, He gives us cheat sheets by illuminating a Bible passage, imparting dreams, unfolding visions, and so forth. He gives us vignettes of things that are about to take place while preparing us for what lies ahead. Now He does not tell us everything, or we wouldn't need the commodities called faith and trust. It is all quite amazing.

I distinctly remember one Sunday morning in May 1975, when I was 22 years old. I was taking one of my regular prayer walks with God, strolling through Pertle Springs Park in Warrensburg, Missouri. Actually voicing the question aloud as though I were talking with a friend walking right beside me, I asked, "Who's for me?" To my utter amazement, an immediate reply came softly right into my heart and mind: "Ann Willard." Somewhat startled, I stuttered, "Who?" Again it came: "Ann Willard."

I reacted at this point: "Well, the last I knew, she was practically engaged to some guy studying to be a Methodist pastor. Who?" Once more the affirming voice of the Lord echoed in the chambers of my heart: "Ann Willard. Not only that, but by September you will be outwardly engaged and the following May 15 you will be married."

I must admit, I did like this news. In fact, I was elated. Ann and I had worked at the local hospital together the summer before and had enjoyed each other's company. As far-fetched as it might sound, it all occurred exactly as it had been spoken. Within four months, Ann Willard and I were outwardly engaged. And on Saturday, May 15, 1976, we were wed. (By the way, our marriage has lasted. At the time of the writing of this book, we have been married for 32 years, praise the Lord.)

I wish it were always that easy. It's not! Before anyone jumps to rash conclusions and makes some blunder, please hold on long enough to read the rest of this book! But this I know with assurance—He is the God of the past, the present and the future. As we hold His hand in a posture of trust and dependency, we can successfully walk the path less chosen, the one on which we can be led by His Holy Spirit in every detail of our lives.

He is the Spirit of Truth, and He always points us in the right direction—toward truth. The Holy Spirit not only gives us a revelation of truth, but He also builds truthfulness into the depths of our personalities. We become like Him as we spend time with Him. His characteristics are imparted to us. They rub off on us, as we've seen it happen in our close relationships. Having the standard of truthfulness built into our lives drops a plumb line into our character, which enables us not only to hear but also to discern the voice of God.

Along with truth, our Helper is willing and able to build into the fabric of our being the many other attributes of God's character. As Tutor, He has personal interest in seeing us grow in expressing what God is like as we express what we hear Him saying.

It Is to Our Advantage

Have you ever needed to know which way to turn? What choice to make? Ever feel like you are caught in the awful position called "transition," where you wonder if things will ever move forward and change? Don't you sometimes wish that a complete guidebook or DVD would just drop down from heaven's storehouse into your lap? Haven't you sometimes wished for a personal appointment with the man Christ Jesus so that He could tell you everything you want to know?

But Jesus said, "It is to your advantage that I go away; for if I do not go away, the Helper shall not come to you; but if I go, I will send Him to you" (John 16:7). Jesus, the Son of God, who cannot lie, told His disciples that its better that the Holy Spirit come and be with you than for Me to remain. Jesus had more things to say to His disciples, but they could not bear them right then. He knew ahead of time that they would need some ongoing coaching. He also knew He would have a lot more disciples to tutor throughout the centuries to come. So the Master enacted a grand plan: He would go back to His Father and they would send the Holy Spirit to the 12 disciples, to the other believers who were with them—and to all subsequent disciples.

That is what He did. After Jesus died, He was buried and He rose from the dead. He ascended into heaven. Then 50 days later, on the Day of Pentecost, the very breath of God came as a mighty wind with tongues of fire. The rest we know as part of our own history. We are witnesses of the fact that He is still blowing that same fire around the world and imparting His Spirit to us today.

God has promised in His Word that He will take care of us and never leave us or forsake us. He knew that when it comes to walking into the shadows of the unknown, we very much prefer to hold someone's hand and be guided by the voice of a wise and strong guide. That's why our Father gave us our very own personal Tutor—His precious Holy Spirit.

Isaiah the prophet declared, "Your ears will hear a word behind you, 'This is the way, walk in it,' whenever you turn to the right or to the left" (Isa. 30:21). Let's begin to learn how to tune in to hear His voice.

Think About It

1. Have you entered into the Spirit-filled life? If not, stop everything and throw yourself into your Savior's arms. Tell Him you want to be entirely His. Ask Him for the gift of His Holy Spirit. He will not disappoint you.

2. Which of the Holy Spirit's special classes are you taking at this time? Are you going through some hard times? Are you enjoying some new opportunities to minister to others? What sets of Scriptures are personally meaningful to you right now? (By the way, don't worry if you seem to repeat some of the lessons you learn. It seems to be part of the normal Christian life.)

Chapter Three

Our Father's Multifaceted Ways

*Behold, an angel of the Lord appeared to Joseph in a dream,
saying, "Arise and take the Child and His mother,
and flee to Egypt, and remain there until I tell you; for Herod
is going to search for the Child to destroy Him."*

MATTHEW 2:13

*And the Lord opened the mouth of the donkey, and she said
to Balaam, "What have I done to you, that you have struck me
these three times?" Then the Lord opened the eyes of Balaam, and
he saw the angel of the Lord standing in the way with his drawn
sword in his hand; and he bowed all the way to the ground.*

NUMBERS 22:28,31

*But He answered and said, "It is written, 'Man shall not
live on bread alone, but on every word that proceeds
out of the mouth of God.'"*

MATTHEW 4:4

After Jesus' 40-day fast, when He was being tempted, Satan said, "If You are the Son of God, command that these stones become bread" (Matt. 4:3). Jesus answered by quoting Deuteronomy 8:3: "Man does not live by bread alone, but man lives by everything that proceeds out of the mouth of the LORD." The word "proceeds," also found in Matthew 4:4, is a continuous action verb. God's life-giving word proceeds and continues to proceed. It is God's ever-proceeding word that gives us life! God has spoken; God is speaking; God will continue to guide His children by speaking.

God has also said that out of the "mouth of two or three witnesses every fact may be confirmed" (Matt. 18:16). For emphasis, we find this statement, or a variation, three times in Scripture: in Deuteronomy 19:15, in Matthew 18:16 and in 2 Corinthians 13:1. Evidently, God wants us to hear His voice, discern it from other voices, and then, through the spirit of wisdom and revelation, correctly interpret and apply the word He has spoken to us.

God does not want us to know only the historical Jesus, who came in human form and walked among men. He greatly yearns that we would also know the living, resurrected Christ through the power of the Holy Spirit. The Father wants to enable us to hear, know and obey the risen Lord. But often we don't realize that He is speaking to us. No wonder we miss His cues. He is such a multifaceted Creator, endlessly creative in how He chooses to communicate.

An Early Lesson

I have never forgotten an early lesson that imprinted my spiritual life. During the Jesus Movement, I was attending a house-church-type meeting. A man from another state was ministering to us young leaders. He was a bit older than I was and he was also more experienced in ministry. I was just sitting on the couch in the living room minding my own business when this man looked straight at me. He said, "Well, you feel like everything's all dried up, don't you?"

Now, at that time, I was not used to being around gifted people who had discernment, people who were capable of prophetically "reading my mail." He continued, "You feel like you're not hearing God's voice right now. Is that right?"

His readout on me was sadly accurate. I had gotten used to hearing God somewhat clearly in one specific way. But often I didn't know what He was saying. The visitor continued, "It's not that God has quit speaking. It's that He has just switched channels on His dial. It's like God uses a radio when He speaks to us. God has not quit speaking to you. He has just turned the knob over to a different channel that you are not used to hearing Him on." This man was using parabolic language; I could understand a radio changing channels. Instead of feeling condemned or exposed, I felt enlightened and encouraged. I *was* hearing God! It's just that there are many different ways the voice of God is transmitted to us. I left the room thinking, *I can't wait to discover the other ways by which my Papa God wants to speak to me!*

Our Father's voice comes to us in such a great variety of ways that we need such moments of enlightenment. Otherwise, we tend to get locked into set patterns. It's so good of God to temporarily shut down one channel in order to open up another. He hasn't quit speaking; He is opening our hearts and minds to hear His voice in new ways. He does this so that we will continue to grow progressively in our relationship with Him. He doesn't want us to become locked in to the same patterns of hearing

Him. God's goal is a real, live relationship with us.

To tell the truth, He likes messing with our radio dial! Sometimes He turns the volume louder and then back down, thus creating a greater dependency on Him. He loves to roll the dial to different stations to help us learn to appreciate the diversity within the Body of Christ. After we have logged a few more listening hours, we are a whole lot less frustrated with who controls the knobs. Eventually, we learn to love the wide variety of ways in which He speaks.

God's Multifaceted Voice

As a good carpenter has more than one tool in his tool chest, so we must have a good assortment of tools available to us in order to properly build the house of the Lord. Here are a few scriptural examples that portray the diversity of tools the Spirit uses to speak to people:

1. A dream or vision (see Job 33:14-18)
2. A voice in a trance (see Acts 10:9-16)
3. The voice of many angels (see Rev. 5:11)
4. The voice of the archangel (see 1 Thess. 4:16)
5. The "sound of many waters" (Rev. 1:15)
6. The sound of the Lord walking in the Garden (see Gen. 3:8)
7. The sound of the army of God marching in the tops of the trees (see 2 Sam. 5:23-25)
8. The audible voice of God (see Exod. 3:4)
9. God "speaking peace" to His people (Ps. 85:8)
10. God's written Word (our primary source of His voice and our chief reference point) (see Ps. 119:105)

11. Wonders in the sky and on Earth (see Joel 2:30-31)
12. Visions and parables to the prophets (see Hosea 12:10)
13. Words and physical metaphors to the prophets (see Jer. 18:1-6)
14. The Holy Spirit speaking to a group (see Acts 13:2)
15. Men, moved by the Holy Spirit, declaring God's voice (see 2 Pet. 1:21)
16. Heavenly experiences in which one is brought up before the Lord (see 2 Cor. 12:1-4)
17. The Holy Spirit bearing witness to our spirit (see Rom. 8:16)
18. A dumb donkey speaking with the voice of a man (see 2 Pet. 2:16)
19. One person speaking the revelatory counsel of the Lord to another (see Jas. 5:19-20)
20. God's own Son (see Heb. 1:2)[1]

This list is not exhaustive, but it gives a bird's-eye view of some of the ways God has chosen to speak to (and through) His people. I have been surprised over the years at both how God speaks and what or whom He chooses to use! Sometimes the package is not one that I would prefer. But He *is* God—and that means He has the right to pick what He wants to say, how to say it and what or whom to use!

God Knows My Number

Once the voice of God came to me in the middle of the night, but I didn't recognize it at first. The ringing of my telephone woke me up. I got up out of bed, went to our kitchen and picked up the phone, only to find there was no one on the other end—just a dial tone. I stumbled back into bed and fell back asleep, only to hear the phone ringing a second time. I rolled out of bed, groped in the dark and picked up the phone, only to find again that there was no voice on the other end.

Wearily, I walked back once more to my bedroom and crawled back into bed, only to be awakened a third time by hearing our telephone ringing. Determined to figure this thing out, I went to the kitchen, picked up the receiver and listened longer. I still didn't hear anything. But this time, a still, small voice in my heart whispered, *Jeremiah 33:3.*

I hung up the receiver, found a Bible and looked up the verse: "Call to Me, and I will answer you, and I will tell you great and mighty things, which you do not know." I was stunned by His invitation, and I spent the next couple of hours just sitting in the quietness of our living room in the presence of the Almighty, communing with Him and listening to His sweet, sweet voice.

Now, folks, that was a genuine God encounter, a personal and unusual way for Him to demonstrate how He takes the initiative to deepen our relationship with Him. He caused the sound of a telephone to awaken me from my sleep. He persisted until He got my full attention. He took me to His written Word. His Word was illuminated by the Holy Spirit and was used to draw me closer to His very bosom. Yes, after He got my attention, I called upon the Lord, and He did show me great and mighty things that I did not previously know!

Quin Sherrer tells us:

God speaks to us in many other ways. If we are open to hearing His voice at every turn, we will begin to recognize it with much greater frequency.[2]

Sherrer continues:

Less dramatically, God can speak to us through an "internal witness" or a "knowing" in our innermost being, a settling peace, a conviction that the decision we might normally fret over is the right one. He can also speak through circumstances ("closed and open doors") or a seemingly serendipitous meeting that brings us an opportunity.[3]

God is not limited in His attention-getting techniques! He wants to be heard, and He has plenty of approaches He can utilize.

Out of the Box

God does not live in a box. He did at one time—but ever since He broke out of the Ark of the Covenant, He has never lived in a box again. Of course, you and I tend to live in boxes that are often fairly nice, although cramped. They're neat, but stuffy. Let's get out of the box! He wants to lift the lid over our head so that we can experience open heavens.

Let's read Psalm 29:3-9 to get a better idea about the variety of ways we might be able to hear the voice of God:

The voice of the LORD is upon the waters; the God of glory thunders, the LORD is over many waters. The voice of the LORD is powerful, the voice of the LORD is majestic. The voice of the LORD breaks the cedars; yes, the LORD breaks in pieces the cedars of Lebanon. And He makes Lebanon skip like a calf, and Sirion like a young wild ox. The voice of the LORD hews out flames of fire. The voice of the LORD shakes the wilderness; the LORD shakes the wilderness of Kadesh. The voice of the LORD makes the deer to calve, and strips the forests bare, and in His temple everything says, "Glory!"

Yes, when the powerful and glorious voice of the Lord comes into our lives, it definitely rolls around in our spirits and "thunders" for a while (v. 3). It really grabs our attention. We can't get away from it and we can't get away from Him. At times, God will manifest Himself as a glorious intruder, as He did with Saul of Tarsus on the road to Damascus. If and when this occurs, we will never be the same. His voice will rock our world!

Majestic and penetrating, the voice of the Lord "breaks the cedars" (v. 5). Cedars are a very dense, hard wood. (Have you ever felt someone was "too dense" for the Lord to reach?) When cedars are broken open, they release an irresistible fragrance. His voice is capable of coming into any situation that looms in front of us like an intimidating giant and mowing it down. Out of that once-foreboding giant, the aroma of Christ can come forth.

Have you ever needed to be refreshed in the Lord? Have you lost some of your zeal along the way? Need to return to your first love? Then God's voice is the cure. The intimacy of His voice will make you skip once again (see v. 6). You will feel like a child at play, ready to run, jump and leap. Your wildness will even return and once again you will learn to love adventure.

Psalm 29 continues, "The voice of the LORD hews out flames of fire" (v. 7). Have any of us ever been scorched by the hot words of God? Sometimes thundering, sometimes quiet and sweet, God's voice can bring intense conviction into our lives. When His authentic fire comes, we may feel like running away from the fire rather than into it. But this fiery word and resulting experience has come to purify us for a useful purpose. Let the fire fall, and let His word purify, cleanse and burn out all of the dross and impurities within our hearts.

Moving on to verse 8, we find that the "voice of the LORD shakes the wilderness." Some of this is pretty uncomfortable. God shakes everything that can be shaken so that that which cannot be shaken will remain. I don't want my life to be built on a foundation that cannot hold up under the pressure. The voice of the Lord will try the foundations of our lives. God makes sure our lives are built upon the solid rock of Jesus Christ and His righteousness. At times of trial, pressure and shaking, we need to let these difficulties propel us to become unshakable.

Do you want creativity to abound in your life? Tired of your own ideas and formulas? Then listen for the voice of the Lord, because it makes the "deer to calve" (v. 9). The voice of the Lord creates faith in the hearer. It changes your circumstances from being barren to being fruitful. My wife and I were diagnosed as medically barren. But the word of the Lord came forth and faith was conceived— and so were four children! We know the voice of the Lord causes the deer to calve! It is never too late for fresh life to emerge. Dormant dreams become activated in a moment by the voice of God. May His word come upon you and cause you to see yourself as a fruitful vine!

"And [the voice of the Lord] strips the forests bare" (v. 9). How do you like that one? God's voice comes, and it removes all the false armor that we rely on. All of our vanities, self-reliance, false images and pretenses are stripped away, and we are left naked before the Creator of the universe. The voice of God brings humility into our lives. According to John 15, it is the tree that has borne fruit that He prunes. So let's be encouraged, looking at the end result and remembering how good He is. If He strips us or asks us to lay something down, He always has a great reason.

He wants us to hear His voice in all of its manifestations so that we can bear much fruit—fruit that will remain.

The End Result

In our process of becoming, we must not forget that ultimately this is not about us. It is about our being transformed into the beautiful image of His glorious Son, Jesus. By the power of the voice of our personal Tutor, the Holy Spirit, you and I will be changed into the image of God's Son. We will shout praises together as we are changed from glory to glory. Everything in His temple says, "Glory!"

Let His voice thunder. Let the fire fall. Let His word be magnified. Let all creation echo His sound. Let His still, small voice continue to proceed. You and I do not live by bread alone but by the ever-proceeding Word of our Father. Yes, everything in His temple shouts "Glory!"

Think About It

1. See if you can list five different ways God's voice came to you—this week! (Think about everything that happened. Do you remember a bit of a dream? Did a verse from the Bible jump off the page at you? Did you experience deep peace? Did your spirit say "amen" to one of the points in your pastor's sermon? Did a friend call to encourage you?)

2. Take some time right now to worship God. Expect Him to draw near to you as you do so.

Chapter Four

Our Kingdom Birthright— Our Kingdom Walk

So then you are no longer strangers and aliens, but you are fellow citizens with the saints, and are of God's household.

EPHESIANS 2:19

But you are a chosen race, a royal priesthood, a holy nation, a people for God's own possession, that you may proclaim the excellencies of Him who has called you out of darkness into His marvelous light.

1 PETER 2:9

And He has made us to be a kingdom, priests to His God and Father; to Him be the glory and the dominion forever and ever. Amen.

REVELATION 1:6

Everyone who is a born-again believer in the Lord Jesus Christ has been translated from the kingdom of darkness into the kingdom of light. We are citizens of a new nation, a holy nation. We are priests in this new Kingdom, and we have the privilege of ministering to God Himself. Whether we are Asian, Russian, Mexican, African, French,

Spanish, British, Chinese, Indian, German, American, Canadian or any other nationality by natural birth, by supernatural birth we are members of the best family, the best bloodline and the best race on the planet. You and I are God's own possession, members of a Chosen Race!

Just as we have rights, privileges and responsibilities that come with our natural citizenship, so it is in the spiritual. As citizens of the kingdom of God, we have rights, privileges and responsibilities to the King of kings and Lord of lords.

A Priest and a Prophet

As full citizens and members of this royal priesthood of the Lord, we have the right to request, at any time, a personal audience with the Master of the Universe. We can come boldly before His throne of grace to bring our requests. As priests, we represent our nations, our neighborhoods, our families and our friends before the throne of Almighty God. We can cast our cares upon the Lord, make intercession on behalf of others or simply come to commune with the lover of our soul.

Just as we have the right as Kingdom citizens to make our appeals before the King, the King has the right to issue commands, decrees, desires and orders to His people. He is more eager than most people realize to exercise His sovereignty, especially when He speaks from heaven to invade our comfort zones, although we can misinterpret His intentions. Sometimes, even the idea that God speaks is too much for us to handle.

In *Surprised by the Power of the Spirit*, Jack Deere writes about how his personal paradigm shifted. He says that the most difficult transition from his old kind of Christianity to a new and improved one was not learning to accept that God heals and does miracles today. Rather, the thing that took the most convincing, that he resisted the most and that he was most afraid of, was accepting that God still *speaks* today.[1]

Yes, God still speaks today, and He has the authority to speak to whomever He wants, whenever He wants, however He wants. As citizens of this Kingdom, we need to know that He wants to speak to us and that it is part of our birthright to be able to hear His voice.

The thing is, His ways are not our ways, so even when we accept that He wants to communicate with us, we have a long-term learning process ahead of us. We all have some unlearning as well as some new learning to do.

Baby Steps

Before a child runs, he or she walks. Before walking comes toddling. Even this half-observant father of four can attest that before toddling comes *falling*. Babies, holding on to anything they can, launch out over and over—then topple or trip back down to the floor. Each of us started this way. The amazing thing is how kids just get up and try to walk again. Babies don't see this falling business as discouraging. The goal—walking—is way too enticing to let a few troubles be a deterrent.

Likewise, no one has a perfect start as he or she learns the Kingdom walk. We all learn by trial and error. However, persistence will be rewarded.

We *will* fall. I can't recount how many times I thought I had heard God, only to find out later that I had missed something important. Of course, I can also look back at some of those times when I thought I must have heard Him incorrectly, only to find out later that I really *had* heard Him correctly after all. It's all part of the learning process. Today, some people acknowledge me as an international prophet. But I had many baby steps along the way.

One such baby step occurred in one of our Jesus People meetings. I thought I was receiving a "word" from God, so I launched out to make it public. The worship had come to a hush; it seemed like the appropriate moment. All ears were directed my way as I blurted out, "Out of your innermost being shall come forth *livers* of living water." The place erupted into laughter. I wanted to find an escape hatch in the floor somewhere so that I could quickly slip out of view! I corrected myself—"I mean *rivers!*"—but it was too late. The *livers* were already out on the table for all to see, never to be stuffed back down again! I really don't recall how the rest of the meeting went. I guess the teacher taught something and the meeting came to a close. But, oh, how I wanted to just go home!

When I did go home, I went to His Word. I found this in Proverbs 24:16: "For a righteous man falls seven times, and rises again." I decided God's people are not quitters and neither was I. The next time out of the stalls, I realized that a bunch of hurdles, such as the fear of man and the fear of rejection, would be standing right in front of me. By the grace of God, I continued to use His gift and respond to His call to convey His word to people, in spite of a few more bleeps and blunders and escapades. Through my mistakes, I learned to hear God's voice and release His word more accurately and effectively.

We all must learn lessons of humility, swallow some pride, seek the Lord for strength and wisdom and move on past mistakes. The important thing is to just *keep moving on*. Making mistakes is not unpardonable. We all have made them, and all will make them in the future. We must learn from our mistakes. We need to turn them over to our Master and let Him use them for His own glory. We can depend on it: All things *do* work together for the good of those who keep on loving God in spite of their temporary setbacks.

It is not always an easy walk or even an easy learning curve. It can be very difficult to find out that we were wrong, especially when we really think we have heard God's voice. Only the Lord's mercy and goodness keep us going as progress comes by trial and error. It's a relationship that we're growing in, not just a set of skills. If we engage the Lord and His will with our whole heart, persistently, we will become proficient in discerning His voice. This is His desire for us, our birthright, the Kingdom walk into which we have been invited.

A Few More Steps—A Few More Lessons

Besides being willing to mess up and to pull ourselves back up whenever we fall, how do we grow in our ability to hear from God? The simplest answer to this question is this: He teaches us one step at a time!

Andy Reese is my neighbor and one of the leaders of my family's church, Grace Center, in Franklin, Tennessee. When Andy teaches about hearing God's voice, he reminds us of how children grow. When we are young in the Lord, our Papa is there to speak to us in ways we can easily understand. Like young children, when we begin to follow Him we need the directions spelled out for us. Andy says that each of us has a sweet spot in our heart. The Holy Spirit knows where it is and how to touch it. He speaks right to it. We melt; we swoon—we are in love. God talks; we hear; we respond. We are on a honeymoon with Jesus and it is great! Then, before we know it, we reduce what God has said into pat equations. But to keep us in a fresh love relationship with God, it seems as if He changes the rules without telling us. We are no longer "babes in Toyland." It can seem that God is no longer speaking at all, or at least He's not speaking in a way we can understand.

We know He loves us. We know He is there—at least we think He is. But the heavens are brass, and it seems that our Papa just isn't interested in us anymore. At those times we think He has gone on vacation or out to lunch. We are tempted to feel, *He used to know my address, but either I moved, He moved or He lost it somewhere!* I call this "When God Seems Silent" or "When the Lollipop Ends."

The truth of the situation is that God is making sure we grow up. Gifts of grace are given in the wet, rainy seasons of life, but the personal character traits we will need in order to carry the gifts are forged in the testing of the desert times. God knows we need both.

By the way, even when we get older in God, those sweet spots in our heart are still there. When He touches one of those areas, we weep, we become a puddle, we're captured once again. He knows how to reel us into His heart.

Papa God speaks to us on our present level while at the same time always prodding us to move on, to grow and to mature. Our Father wants us to reach higher levels. To do so, we can't keep communicating at our familiar level. We can't forever be talking baby talk, so to speak.

We must make another shift, go through another time of growth and take another lesson in His language of love. We must embrace another opportunity to exercise faith in the reality that He is with us whether we "feel" His presence or not. He has promised never to leave us or forsake us, and we can take that one to the bank any day of the week. I love to feel His presence, but my faith in Him is not based on how much I feel. It is based on His Word of promise. His name is Emmanuel—God with us.

His loving desire to be in communication with us never ebbs or ceases. We will soon find out that we are the ones who need to change. We are the ones who must lean into His heart to hear His sweet love language. "When I was a child, I used to speak as a child, think as a child, reason as a child; when I became a man, I did away with childish things" (1 Cor. 13:11).

Speaking Less and Listening More

We can't leapfrog down the road the fast way; rather, learning to hear God takes time. Hearing God takes patience, too. If we don't realize this, we won't set aside enough time to listen, to seek Him or to inquire of Him. Our Western society does not teach us the art of listening. But the connection is obvious: If we want to hear, we must listen. I recommend speaking a little less and listening a whole lot more. Here is another hint: If we don't make time, He will help us to make time. He knows how to get our attention.

My personal Tutor has taught me many lessons about this. For example, over the years, I have been awakened in the middle of the night hundreds if not thousands of times. At first I did not understand what was going on. I tried (unsuccessfully) to just turn over in bed and go back to sleep. I rebuked sleep disorders: "Get out of here in Jesus' name!" But it didn't work. It took a while to figure out what He wanted me to do, which was to wait up and watch with Him for a while, after which I could do what I wanted to do—sleep!

Over a period of time, I learned to get up out of bed (highly important—get *out* of the bed!) in the middle of the night and go sit in my recliner chair in our living room. I didn't do a lot of heavy intercession or spiritual burden-bearing—I was just there. For a while I thought I was wasting both God's time and my own. But eventually I learned the lesson: All He wanted was me. He simply wanted a friend, a companion, a lover with whom He could share His heart. I have learned more about His voice in the wee hours of the morning than any other time. Now I love being on call to be with Him. It is a privilege to be called and chosen to be His friend.

During the quiet hours of the night, I have learned to turn the ear of my spirit in His direction. One of the most common ways I hear from the Lord is simply by hearing the quiet inner voice of the Holy Spirit. God can and does speak to me in many ways, but He comes to me most often through His peaceful inner voice communing with my heart.

As a mother trains her ear to hear her babe, even when she's asleep, we need to train our ears to hear the slightest whisper from God. It will take time and repetition, but with the help of the Holy Spirit, who really is our private personal Tutor, we can learn how to pay attention. We need to make the effort, take the time and set aside portions of our days or nights. He greatly desires to help us and empower us. Hearing God's voice just won't happen automatically. If we take time to be with Him, we will hear what the Lord our God is speaking. I guarantee it.

There's Going to Be a Revolution!

About 40 years ago, a new sound broke forth from England and it quickly swept the world: A singing group called the Beatles took the nations by storm. Their simple, catchy lyrics captured hearts and promoted changes. One of their top songs was "Revolution." It helped throw an impressionable generation into a wild frenzy of drugs, free love and rebellion against authority.

Forty years later another new sound can be heard. Another generation of people is discontented with the status quo. A radical yet intimate sound of prayer and worship is invading the Church and beginning to make a worldwide impact. I believe we are on the verge of a societal prophetic revolution, a dramatic shift. Watch out, world; watch out, slumbering Church! This sleepy Bride is about to shake off her passivity, arise and become all that God has destined her to be. A clarion call to change and intimacy is ringing across the land. Draft notices are being sent out from heaven: Wanted—Passionate, Consecrated Warriors.[2]

Great change is coming. But first, great change must come to us in our own personal walks with God. When this happens, if and only when this happens, then great change will suddenly appear in the global Body of Christ. My heart echoes the cries of Michael Brown, theologian and leader of the FIRE Schools on the east coast of the United States. In his radical book *Revolution! The Call to Holy War*, he declares:

> Why is this dedication to a cause—this passionate, often selfless, sometimes murderous, always fanatical dedication—characteristic of revolutionary movements? It is because the revolutionary has an unshakable conviction that something is terribly wrong with society, that something very important is missing, that something major needs to change, indeed, that it must change now.[3]

Sam Storms, teacher, author and present faculty member of Wheaton College, trumpets similar thoughts in his book *The Beginner's Guide to Spiritual Gifts*:

> I want you to be expectant about what God can do for you and for those he's called you to help with his power. I want your faith and confidence in both God's goodness and his greatness to grow and intensify. Skeptics about what God can do will rarely experience his power.[4]

Let's dare to believe that when we ask for directions we will receive them. Let's start out by changing our expectations and looking for the blueprints that God wants to release. Let's believe that the Holy Spirit is our personal

Tutor and that He has plans for our lives. Let's believe that we have a Kingdom birthright to hear from God. Let's believe that God actually does hear our prayers!

God really does want us to hear His voice more than we want to hear it. As our Father, He wants to speak to His children. Let every day be Father's Day. Honor Him. Listen to Him. Let's do what He tells us to do.

Are you beginning to be a believing believer? Are you engaging your spirit to expect to receive revelation from God? Before you know it, you will be hearing His present-day voice in your life and you will be passing on your contagious passion to others.

Think About It

1. Have you said, "Help, I've fallen, and I can't get up"? Turn those words into a prayer:

   Help, Lord, I've fallen and I need Your help to get back up.

2. Earlier in your Christian walk, were you able to hear God's voice more than you do now? How can you respond to His invitation to listen for His words?

Chapter Five

Our Road Map

Thy Word is a lamp to my feet, and a light to my path.
PSALM 119:105

Be diligent to present yourself approved to God as a workman who does not need to be ashamed, handling accurately the word of truth.
2 TIMOTHY 2:15

Let the word of Christ dwell in you richly.
COLOSSIANS 3:16, *NKJV*

I have traveled thousands of miles in recent years, criss-crossing many nations by airplane, train and automobile. Scores of times, what has helped me to get to the right place at the right time is a good road map, either printed or electronic. Turning on my cell phone to check in with the right person at the last minute has saved my neck more than once. Though I am sensitive in my spiritual orientation, I tend naturally to be one who gets lost rather easily. Those who know me well call me direction-ally challenged. I need all the help I can get.

God has not left us on our own, *map*less or helpless, to try to figure out how to get to His destinations. He has given us our personal Tutor, the Holy Spirit, to guide us into all truth. He has also given us His road map of life, the Word of God. This manual spells out in plain print much of our most desperately needed direction. But as with any road map, it won't do us much good if we keep it stuffed away in our glove box or on a shelf collecting dust. We have to take it out and use it.

If we haven't read our Bible, we should not act like we know where we are going. Without it, we could take a wrong turn on the road and double the length of time it takes to get to our destination. We need to get smart! We need to take out the map and study it so that we get to know the territory we are entering. We will need to review the road map many times, in order to end up at the right place without running out of gas or even running off the road. To complete our journey with the Lord, we must study, read and meditate on the written Word of God. As we read it and chew on it, His Word will begin to dwell richly in our heart and mind, and we will reach the destination He has planned for our lives.

My Companion and Friend

Like most pastors, I own several editions of the greatest Book ever written. But there is one in particular that has been my daily companion for more than 20 years. It is torn; it falls apart often; it has been round the world with me. My favorite Bible is marked full of love notes from my kids, such as the one our third child, Tyler, sent me when he was about three years old. Innocently, he tore Isaiah 42 and 43 to shreds. My wife quickly gathered up the fragments of those favorite chapters of mine, taped the little pieces all back together and, before I got home, stuck them back in my Bible where they belonged. They are still that way today—and I love it! A bit later, little Rachel, our fourth child, decided to draw pictures for me in 1 Peter, in red ink. Her scribbles are there today, and I love every blot!

Once while I was on staff with Metro Christian Fellowship in Kansas City, I was in one of the upstairs offices doing some prayer counseling. I always took my favorite Bible with me just in case I needed to give a Scripture to someone as a bit of medicine for what might be ailing him or her. But after that appointment, I could not find my favorite brown leather *New American Standard Bible* for days, so I used other Bibles. They were okay. But I felt a bit lost. My personal Bible contained sermon notes I had written when I had heard the teachings of Mike Bickle, Paul Cain, Francis Frangipane, Jack Deere, and many others. Where did my Bible go? I cried out to the Lord, "Where is my Bible?"

For many days, I used what I call the Necessary in Vineyard Bible—the *New International Version* (*NIV*). I chomped on the *New King James*. I tried huffing down the original *King James Version*. All are great versions, but I did not feel right without my familiar version. After about four weeks of this, I wandered back upstairs in the Metro office building to the same room where I had had my appointment. There was my brown leather Bible lying on the carpet! I gleefully exclaimed, "I found my friend! I found my lost friend!" I was beside myself with joy. I felt the Holy Spirit was pleased that I was so pleased. It's the Word of God, so much more than a book of doctrine, history and good teaching, and it just didn't taste the same if I wasn't chewing on my favorite copy. I had been as lost as if some-one had switched road signs on me.

Do you have a "close friend" Bible, one with words you can hide in your heart readily, one you can chew on? I read my favorite Bible—and it reads me! It is the only book ever written that is not just ink on page—it is alive and active, sharper than any two-edged sword (see Heb. 4:12).

Store Up the Word of God

We are admonished to hide God's Word in our heart. As we do this consistently, we establish safety, security and protection for our lives. We then have a basis from which to judge the multitude of voices that come our way. We have a vast well of His words to draw from in times of need.

There's a direct correlation between *hearing* and *hiding* the Word of God within our heart and mind. Both are keywords, action words.

I grew up in a rural community, where my mother was famous for her canned produce, which she had grown in our large garden. She would often put up a hundred quarts of green beans and dozens of pints of corn, homemade pickles and even bottles of grape juice. In the heat of the Midwest summer, she would get out her pressure cooker in our little kitchen to produce food that would feed her family during the winter ahead. When winter set in, we were glad that Mom had invested so much time storing up in a time of plenty for a time of need.

Just as my mother stored up fruit, vegetables and produce to be used, eaten and enjoyed at a later date, so we store up the written Word of God (*logos* in Greek) so it later can be "eaten" as a life-producing spoken word (*rhema* in Greek). Through reading, studying, repeating, memorizing, praying and meditating on the written Word, we accumulate an enormous resource in our mind and heart that can be submitted to the Holy Spirit's transforming power. A quickening work of God occurs and the written logos becomes activated into a present-tense, spoken, rhema word of God.

Comparing Logos and Rhema

The term "logos" (written word) is used 331 times in the Greek New Testament. The word "rhema" (spoken word) is used more than 70 times in the New Testament. "Logos" is used well over four times as often as is "rhema," which helps us to see the relative importance of the logos, the sure foundation, the written Word of God.

Vine's Expository Dictionary of New Testament Words states:

> The significance of rhema as distinct from logos is exemplified in the injunction to take up the sword of the Spirit which is the Word of God, or the spoken rhema word used in Ephesians 6:17. Here the reference is not to the whole Bible as such but to an individual Scripture which the spirit brings to our remembrance for our use in a time of need, a prerequisite being the regular storing of the mind with the Scripture.[1]

Below are some further differentiations that also show the relationship between the written Word of God and the spoken word:

1. *Planning and the execution.* Logos is that which is in the mind before communication occurs. Rhema is the vocalization, the articulation involved in expression. Logos is the thinking and rhema is the saying. Logos signifies the thought and rhema emphasizes the speaking.

2. *Message and the vehicle.* Logos connotes the planning and the purpose. Rhema represents the execution of the plan or its oral expression. Logos is the content; rhema is the vehicle for the context. Rhema emphasizes a spoken message or the preached gospel, while logos stresses the message itself.

3. *Whole and the part.* Logos can signify the whole speech, the entire message or the complete doctrine. The rhema can represent the individual supporting arguments. Logos tends toward the whole, while rhema means a specific part of the total word.

If we want to move in the inspirational rhema element of the Word, we must store up the logos content of the Word. We can't have one without the other!

Hearing the Word Releases Faith

We read many things, but do we always really hear what we read? Romans 10:17 tells us, "Faith comes from hearing [acoa in Greek], and hearing by the word [rhema] of

Christ." "Acoa" means to have audience with, to come with ears.

This is vitally important. The inner attitude of our heart will determine whether we've heard what is being stated. In other words, we can read the written Word and leave unchanged. But if we approach the Word of God with the correct inner attitude of the heart by coming with ears ready to listen, we will give full attention to the Word, have an audience with it and leave changed. If we come with a heart of submission, expecting to receive like a child or student from his or her caring parent or teacher, we will receive much.

How do we develop these important inner attitudes and expectancies that will determine how we hear and thus what we receive? Glancing again at Romans 10:17—"Faith comes from hearing"—we see that our faith comes and continues to come by having an ongoing audience with God's words through the fellowship of the Holy Spirit.

Our faith quickens us, energizes us, releases and motivates us to take action. It requires the written Word and the spoken word, the logos and the rhema, to be brought together by the Spirit of God, who activates and releases the effect of God's Word, creating faith in our lives. I want to receive and exercise faith. I know that faith pleases God. It enables me to live in new life. So, if I want to hear God's voice, I must come to God with my ears on.

Meditating on the Word of Life

We can read the Word. We can pray based on the words we read. But the approach to the Scriptures that will best

help us to turn the logos into rhema is the spiritual disci-
pline of *meditating* on the Word of Life.

In *Wasted on Jesus,* I attempted to dust off the art of meditation and give some clarity to it. I wrote that the word "meditate" means to think deeply, or to reflect on something. To
"reflect" on something means to contemplate or ponder it.
"Contemplate" means to gaze at or think about intensely.[2]

These words are slow, careful words. When we are meditating on Scripture, it is not so much the amount of text
we read as what we chew. It may be no more than a single
verse. It may only be a few words such as "as the deer pants
for the water" (Ps. 42:1). Peter Toon, author of *Meditating as
a Christian*, writes, "Meditation is . . . taking to heart, reading slowly and carefully, prayerfully taking in, and humbly
receiving into mind, heart, and will that which God has revealed . . . by the indwelling Spirit of Christ."[3]

I often turn to the contemporary writings of Richard
Foster, a brilliant author and writer on spiritual disciplines.
In *Prayer: Finding the Heart's True Home*, he writes:

> In Meditative Prayer the Bible ceases to be a quo-
> tation dictionary and becomes instead "wonderful
> words of life" that lead us to the Word of Life. It
> differs even from the study of Scripture. Whereas
> the study of Scripture centers on exegesis, the med-
> itation upon Scripture centers on internalizing and
> personalizing the passage. The written Word be-
> comes a living word addressed to us.[4]

Meditation is an awesome tool to aid all of us as believers in hearing the voice of God. Let's chew on the Word
of God. It is our daily bread.

Gathering Our Manna

The children of Israel had manna as their daily bread when they wandered in the wilderness. It was bread from heaven.

> Then the LORD said to Moses, "Behold, I will rain bread from heaven for you; and the people shall go out and gather a day's portion every day, that I may test them, whether or not they will walk in My instruction. And it will come about on the sixth day, when they prepare what they bring in, it will be twice as much as they gather daily."
>
> In the morning there was a layer of dew around the camp. When the layer of dew evaporated, behold, on the surface of the wilderness there was a fine flake-like thing, fine as the frost on the ground. When the sons of Israel saw it, they said to one another, "What is it?" For they did not know what it was. And Moses said to them, "It is the bread which the Lord has given you to eat" (Exod. 16:4-5,13-15).

The Israelites didn't know what the flake-like things were. Many times God's voice or even provision comes in a way that we do not instantly identify as such. We do not readily recognize the answers to our very own prayers. We respond, "What is this? That can't be God!"

The story continues in verses 16 to 19:

> This is what the LORD has commanded, "Gather of it every man as much as he should eat; you shall take an omer apiece according to the number of

persons each of you has in his tent." And the sons of Israel did so, and some gathered much and some little. . . . He who had gathered much had no excess, and he who had gathered little had no lack; every man gathered as much as he should eat. And Moses said to them, "Let no man leave any of it until morning."

But some did not follow Moses' orders, and they left part of it until the next day and it bred worms. When the Israelites obeyed the Lord's commandments, every family had all that they needed. When they obeyed, the manna did not spoil.

Real-Life Applications

We must gather the Word as manna every day. Our portion today is only good for today. We cannot live off yesterday's manna. If we do not eat today's portion, we will have lack and need. But if we abide in His Word daily, we will have life within. That's the basic message here. We cannot live life today on yesterday's Word. By the same token, we cannot expect presumptuously to hear God's rhema today when we haven't gathered in His logos yesterday or last week or last month, chewing it and digesting it. We can't get God's voice activated in our life without first putting it into our heart and mind.

It's an issue of obedience. Each of us needs to gather his or her own manna, although we may gather and eat it together, in each other's company.

Once I was praying for someone, and I was about to jump in and solve his problem for him. Suddenly, it was as if the Holy Spirit had slapped my hand and said to me, "Don't put the spoon in his mouth! Put it in his hand and teach him how to feed himself." We must equip and teach each other the necessities of spiritual disciplines such as reading and meditating on Scripture. There is no substitute!

If we want to end up at the right place at the right time to see the written Word turn into an immediate word from God, if we want faith that pleases God, and if we want to hear His sweet voice—get out a road map, read it and follow the directions. We will surely make it to the end of our journey with manna to spare, just as the Israelites experienced every Sabbath when the extra food they had gathered didn't spoil as it did on the other days.

The Word of God—it's your road map for the journey of life. And the One who wrote it, the Holy Spirit, is your personal Tutor, waiting to speak a word into your ear: "This is the way, walk in it" (Isa. 30:21).

Think About It

1. Why does God's spoken word depend on His written Word? In your personal experience, can you point to a time when you may have bypassed this connection?

2. Do you take time every day to gather manna from Scripture? What can you do to grow in this area?

Chapter Six

Our Practical Tools

*Therefore everyone who hears these words of Mine, and acts
upon them, may be compared to a wise man, who built his
house upon the rock. And the rain descended, and the floods
came, and the winds blew, and burst against that house; and yet
it did not fall, for it had been founded upon the rock.*

MATTHEW 7:24-25

Thus far in this book we have been laying a firm foundation for our house of God to be built upon. It is time now to learn from Jesus, our Master Carpenter, how to use a few tools (principles) that can assist us in the art of hearing and following God's voice. This chapter is very pragmatic.[1]

1. Don't Make It Complicated!

It is not hard to hear God. We tend to overcomplicate the whole matter. The following three simple steps will help us hear God's gracious voice:

Step One: Submit to His lordship. Let's ask Him to help silence our own thoughts, desires and opinions. We want to hear only the thoughts of the Lord. Take the advice that is given in Proverbs 3:6-7: "In all your ways acknowledge Him, and He will make your paths straight. Do not be wise in your own eyes; Fear the LORD and turn away from evil."

George Müller was an Englishman, one of the great evangelical champions of the faith. He lived this first principle. By faith alone, he supported vast orphanages. He would pray daily for the provisions to feed these hundreds of children who were under his care. One of the secrets in George Müller's walk with God was so simple, yet it is rarely taught today: He told his followers that if they wanted to hear from God and pray in faith, then they first would have to cleanse themselves of their own opinions. Another word for this is "submission."

We can't hear God if we have a preformed opinion on an issue. We must submit to His lordship. We need to consciously submit our thoughts, our opinions, our preconceived attitudes and notions, and even our traditions, to the Lord.

Step Two: Resist the enemy. We can use the authority Jesus Christ has given us as His disciples to silence the voice of the enemy. We can stand firm in our position as God's own children. We need to learn what it means to apply the blood of Jesus over our lives. We can resist the enemy, who comes to our mind with all sorts of fears and plausible doubts. God's Spirit in us will make us able to do what we can never do solo, and Jesus' powerful name will convince Satan to leave.

The apostle James wrote, "Submit therefore to God. Resist the devil and he will flee from you" (4:7). Submit first; then resist.

Step Three: Ask a question and expect God's answer. We should ask the very question that is in our heart, bringing it before the throne of Almighty God. Then we need to wait for Him to answer. We should not expect to get an answer to pop right up ("You've got mail!"); rather, we should wait expectantly, believing that as we have submitted to God and resisted the enemy, we will be "filled with the knowledge of His will in all spiritual wisdom and understanding" (Col. 1:9). At times, an immediate reply may come. The vital third step after submitting and resisting is to *expect* God to act.

2. Allow God to Speak However He Chooses

We should not try to dictate to God the guidance methods we prefer; rather, we must listen with a yielded heart. There is a direct link between yielding and hearing. He may choose to speak to us in a method that we are not accustomed to. He can speak through His written Word, through a person, through dreams or visions, or through a quiet inner voice. Having submitted to Him, resisted the enemy and asked for an answer, we should not dictate the way we want Him to respond to our request. Let's receive grace from His storehouse, the grace of expectant yielding. We need to always allow God to speak in the way He chooses.

3. Confess Any Known Sins

A clean heart is a prerequisite to hearing God. We read in Psalm 66:18: "If I regard wickedness in my heart, the Lord will not hear." If the Lord doesn't even hear us, then we're not going to receive the answer that we're hoping for—because He hasn't even heard the question yet. The third tool for hearing God's voice is foundational to the ABCs of Christianity—the confession of sins. We need to confess our sins to our Father in Jesus' great name. He is waiting to forgive us.

4. Obey the Last Thing God Said

Why would God give us new orders if we haven't obeyed His last ones? He's waiting for us to do what He's already told us to do. This alone could be a primary roadblock. If He has already spoken, and we already know what is required of us, then we should go do it—for Jesus' sake! It's an issue of obedience.

These principles are laid out in the story about Elisha the prophet and the servant who was rigorously chopping down some trees with which to expand the place where they were living.

> So he went . . . to the Jordan, [and] they cut down trees. But as one was felling a beam, the axe head fell into the water; and he cried out and said, "Alas, my master! For it was borrowed." Then the man of God said, "Where did it fall?" And when he showed him the place, he cut off a stick, and threw it in there, and made the iron float. And he said, "Take it up for yourself." So he put out his hand and took it (2 Kings 6:4-7).

Here is the Goll paraphrase:

The servant has been working away cutting down trees with his axe. It seems that all of a sudden he flies off the handle—oops, I mean the axe head does! He loses his head and flies off the handle. The servant lost relationship with the head.

Now here's the reality: An axe head does not become loosened up all at once. This occurs over time due to neglect. The cutting edge grows dull. When the cutting edge is not resharpened, after the axe is used for a job, eventually the woodcutter needs to put more of his strength into every swing. He still gets productivity, but each time there ends up being a little more of his strength and a little duller edge. Over time, the axe head becomes terribly dull. It loses its tight fit with the handle. When it eventually falls off the handle, it seems to happen all of a sudden, but really we know better. If it can happen that way in the natural, it also can happen that way in the spiritual.

We need to tend to our axe head, keeping it sharp. We should make sure that our relationship is right with the Head of the Body of Christ and confess our sins daily. We should not wait six months before asking the Holy Spirit to turn on His lights inside for an inspection; rather, we need to do that every day! In my own relationship with the Holy Spirit, I often sanctify three days of fasting just for the purpose of cleansing my heart. I'm not asking God for stuff; I'm asking God to tenderize my heart. Knowing that I still sin and realizing that sin makes me lose my edge and that it loosens my connection with the Lord, I need to take a maintenance break. Like anyone else, I can end up putting too much of my own strength into situations, and as a result, my head can get lost in the field of my labors. I may even fly off the handle. Then (good news!), the Son of God comes along and says to me, "Ah, I see you lost your head. You flew off the handle, eh? Where did it fall?" And when I show Him the exact place, my cutting edge will be summoned. It's as much of a miracle as an iron axe head that floats—I am restored, complete and useful.

What is the key for receiving back the cutting edge? We must point out the place where we lost it. We must go back to the place where we heard and haven't yet obeyed. "God is opposed to the proud, but gives grace to the humble" (Jas. 4:6; 1 Pet. 5:5). The condition for grace has just been met.

When in humility we point out our place of falling, He takes a stick (a symbol of the cross) and He throws the wood of the cross of Jesus into the place of our failure, and a miracle happens! We don't have to conjure up some religious performance; the voice of God is back. We have been restored. He is within us. The axe head surfaces, and it comes back to the shore on the waves, to be restored to its proper place of usefulness.

5. Get Your Own Leading

God will use others to confirm our guidance, but we must learn to hear the voice of the Lord for ourselves. God is a jealous God. That means He wants to talk with us personally. We need to become secure in our own identity in Christ. We must realize that we are sons and daughters of the Creator of the universe and that He wants to relate to us in our own right. We should not be wrongly codependent on others. At the same time, we should not jump the tracks by cultivating an independent and rebellious spirit. We need to hear God for ourselves.

6. Don't Talk About Your Word Too Soon

This is a really helpful tool. I wish I had known this one a bit earlier in my life! I think the dreamer Joseph might have wished he had heard this one too! Waiting helps us avoid not-so-obvious pitfalls. When God tells us something, it's as if He is sharing a secret with a trusted friend. We should consider asking permission before opening wide our mouth and repeating everything we supposedly know. Here are four traps I have discovered:

The Trap of Pride

Just because we've heard the Lord doesn't mean that we have developed the character to carry out the action. We might think, *Man, am I a hotshot! I heard God today.* We center more around ourselves and our gifts instead of the Master and His ways, becoming prideful.

The Trap of Presumption

Presumption makes us act as if we know it all. After all, we've heard God! Could it be that we heard only part of what God wanted to say? One portion could be coming through some life experiences and another part through other people. We need to pray for the word we hear to be informed by a living understanding of how and when to act. We should stay humble, remembering that even though we are special to God, we aren't the only spokespeople He has.

The Trap of Missed Timing

There is a *kairos* moment (perfect timing) for all things. If we talk about our word too soon, we might miss the Savior's timing and end up attempting to fulfill our word with second-rate results. We should remember what happened to Abraham and not birth an Ishmael because we just *couldn't wait* for an Isaac.

The Trap of Confusion

"God is not the author of confusion" (1 Cor. 14:33, *NKJV*). Premature public chatting about all we have heard in private can result in confusion for ourselves as well as for others. To avoid the trap of confusion, we can set a guard over our heart and mouth and speak only those things that build up our hearers.

Oftentimes, God does tell us something ahead of time, before it comes into being. His word comes to prepare us and to change us to be the vessel qualified to do what has been spoken. We all seem to need to learn the hard way not to talk out of turn.

7. Know That God Will Confirm What He's Telling You

God will give us our own stuff—there is plenty to go around, but we can depend on the fact that God does use others to confirm His word. It's a part of His safety net of protection (2 Cor. 13:1: "Every fact is to be confirmed by the testimony of two or three witnesses"). If it really is God speaking, He will speak the same or similar thing more than once. I sigh with relief over that one. It helps to take the pressure off. In other words, you and I don't have to try to figure out what to do with a one-time word! If it really is from God, it will be confirmed. We can rest in that fact.

We can trust that the Lord will speak through those in authority over us. If we are children living with our parents, we should pray for them. We can pray for our elders and pastors and those who are over them. A married woman should pray for her husband to have wisdom. Everyone should pray for those with whom they are going to take counsel. We need to bathe each situation in prayer. We can ask the Lord for trusted channels of authority in our life by which we can receive correction, encouragement, admonition and confirmation of what we believe God is saying. God will confirm His word to us through others. There is safety in many counselors (see Prov. 15:22).

8. Beware of Counterfeits

Satan loves to counterfeit. He is not the Creator, so he has no originality; he's just a copycat! Think about what a counterfeit means. It implies that there's something authentic and real out there, something worth copying. There is counterfeit money because there's real money, and it has power.

The enemy counterfeits God's voice and he counterfeits experiences, even rare supernatural experiences. Why are the psychic hotlines so popular? Why does the New Age movement seem to have so much influence? People turn to psychics and New Age thinking because they so hungrily want to encounter the supernatural. People want guidance. People are born with a void that only the voice of God can fill. You want to hear His voice, or you wouldn't be reading this book.

But beware of counterfeits from the dark side. Our vigilance is an important part of our equipment. While we remain vigilant, we can find reassurance in the fact that the very existence of counterfeit guidance proves that the Lord of hosts, who has the real power, also has the real thing: the real voice, the real dreams, myriad real angels and the true guidance system.

9. Practice Hearing God's Voice

Yes, practice hearing the voice of God, and it will become easier. It's like picking up the phone and recognizing the voice of a friend, whose voice you know because you've heard it so many times. Years ago, I learned a lesson about this the hard way.

I am the youngest of three children. My oldest sister is six years older than I, and by the time I was in high school, she was long gone out of the home. Naturally, I did not know her very well. Later, when I was at college, the phone rang one night and I went out into the dorm hallway to answer it. There was an unfamiliar woman's voice on the other end of the phone: "Well hello, James. How are you?"

"I'm fine. Uh, who is this?"

It was the voice of my older sister, Sandra, but I did not recognize it. I think it might have hurt her a bit that I did not recognize the voice of a member of my own family. I determined that I needed to get to know her voice before she called again!

If I want to know the voice of the Holy Spirit, I've got to spend some time with Him. When I said, "Uh, who is this?" I felt a tiny bit of what the Holy Dove of God so often feels when He is overlooked and unrecognized. I want the voice of the Holy Spirit to become lovely to me. I never want to grieve Him. (By the way, I have a wonderful relationship with my older sister now because I know her dear voice and the heart with which she speaks.)

Get to know the voice of your Master by spending time "on the phone" with Him. Practice makes perfect.

10. Cultivate an Intimate Relationship

From God's perspective, the most important reason for hearing the voice of God is not so that we will know the right things to do but so that we will know Him, the source of the guidance.

True guidance involves getting closer to the Guide. We grow to know the Lord better as He speaks to us. As we listen to Him and obey His Word, our relationship with Him goes far beyond information, guidance, dreams, visions, angels and all the other wonderful supernatural stuff. The gifts of the Spirit are appetizers to whet our desire for more of God Himself. The voice of God creates a deeper hunger within us so that we might come into closer communion with Him. The primary reason we need to hear His voice is really simple: to cultivate the intimate relationship with our Abba Father that He wants us to have. Our Daddy wants to commune with us even more than we want to commune with Him. Draw near, for He draws near to us.

Think About It

1. Which of these 10 tools do you need most to learn how to use? Which do you need to pick up right now?

2. Which of these tools do you find easiest to use? Why?

Chapter 7

Our Brothers, Our Sisters

*If the foot should say, "Because I am not a hand, I am not a
part of the body," it is not for this reason any the less a part of
the body. And if the ear should say, "Because I am not an eye,
I am not a part of the body," it is not for this reason any the less
a part of the body. If the whole body were an eye, where would
the hearing be? If the whole were hearing, where would the
sense of smell be? But now God has placed the members,
each one of them, in the body, just as He desired.*

1 CORINTHIANS 12:15-18

*A new commandment I give to you, that you love one another,
even as I have loved you, that you also love one another.
By this all men will know that you are My disciples,
if you have love for one another.*

JOHN 13:34-35

Have you ever noticed the assortment of Christians at
a large church gathering, a conference or a rally? As you
scanned the crowd, have you dared to wonder what it will
be like spending time in heaven with all those folks? Awesome, right? Uh, now let's get real—there sure seem to be
a lot of peculiar odds and ends out there. The funny
thing is, these just happen to be our brothers and sisters

in Christ. What will it be like to spend eternity with them? Or (gulp!) try to imagine spending eternity with the people you really know well.

There are occasions, I must admit, when I am judgmental of some of God's chosen ones and, even worse, critical. Sometimes I look at the outside wrapper and swallow hard. I don't even know them and find myself already having a hard time with them. Yet I know that I will be spending eternity with them, and they with me, in heaven. By the grace of God, I will have His love for each and every one. I can't claim to have it yet.

Each one of us is a jewel in the eyes of our Papa God. His Son, Jesus, loved us so much that He died for each one of us. Sometimes it's the most basic truths that we tend to forget.

Philip asked Jesus to show the disciples the Father (see John 14:8). Imagine the Son of God's disappointment, maybe even hurt, knowing they hadn't yet gotten the picture. In essence He answers, "Hey, Philip, in case you didn't realize it in these past three years, the Father has been right here before you. If you have seen who I am, and if you have watched the works I have done, you have seen the Father" (see John 14:9). What had they witnessed? They had seen Him touch the lame and blind with compassion. They had seen Him hold the children in His arms. They had witnessed His tears. Whether He was healing, teaching, comforting or raising the dead, Jesus always exemplified the Father.

We are called to be witnesses, light and salt in this world. We are His children, and we are supposed to look, act and talk like Him as His representatives on Earth. But is the world able to see the Father's love in us? Moreover, can we see and hear our Papa God in and through our brothers and sisters?

God Will Speak Through All of His Children

One of the most common ways the Lord speaks is through the members of the Body of Christ—each and every one. I think God must have a lot of flat-out fun at times as He attempts to speak to us through our spouses, parents, children, neighbors and other odds and ends besides the ones we believe He is supposed to speak through. We accept the fact that our pastor or favorite Bible teacher at a conference or our church hears from God. But does God speak through Jerry, Susie or (fill in the name)? Each of us is so different. He made us that way. The Holy Spirit must find it a bit hard and yet fun and a little crazy sometimes to speak through all these different and unique vessels.

God loves diversity. He created all of life to display His passion for variety and His personal touch. We must be aware of this bent if we are to learn to hear Him through our brothers and our sisters. We each have our own quirks, comfort zones and preferences. Certain teachers talk our lingo. Some people just push all of our buttons the right way. We love to hear God's latest word through these people—and then there are the others. In all our lives there will be the others, the ones who punch our buttons upside-down and ring our doorbells without mercy. Guess what? God Himself just might be at the door, and in our aggravation, we might miss Him.

Paul covers this tendency in 1 Corinthians 12:12-27. The Body of Christ has a diversity of parts, each one important to the whole. And yet the eye chatters to the foot, "Hey, I can't receive from you, you're not a part of my comfort zone." Why? "You're one of those 'renewal people.'" The ear tells the knee, "Your church label has no room for what I've got to offer." The wrist declares to the hand, "Listen, honey, I'm the head of this house. I'm the spiritual leader here. I can move you any way I want. You just sit there and let me do the leading."

We all do it. We set our own strict little boundaries about how and through whom God can speak to us. We make a select list. Then, wham, somebody messes with our list. We don't know what hit us, so we rebuke the devil. Later on, after we've become more humble, we learn it was God. Sometimes I wonder if He actually delights in messing with our lives, doctrines and perimeters. I know He has worked me over a few times.

Invasion

In 1992, the presence of the Lord invaded our house. His angels came. His presence was manifested in startling ways. At 11:59 P.M. on the Jewish Day of Atonement, a heavenly visitor came and stood in our bedroom and spoke to me as the clock turned to midnight. "I have come to speak with your wife," the visitor said. Not to me, mind you, but to my sweet wife, Michal Ann. The ensuing weeks of unusual divine encounters rocked our world, and the reverberations are still being felt today.

In *Encounters with a Supernatural God*, Michal Ann tells about this profound experience:

Beginning on the Day of Atonement, October 6, 1992, our family entered a nine-week period of supernatural visitations that forever changed our lives—especially mine. In retrospect, I suppose that period was like a compressed "pregnancy" in the spirit, measured in weeks instead of months. All I know is that by the time it was over, God had birthed a whole new identity in me that literally changed my relationship with Jim and revolutionized our approach to ministry.[1]

Those were interesting days indeed. When I went out on the road ministering, I would call home to find out what God was saying! Here I had a certain reputation of being the one who could hear what the Lord was saying—but my wife? It was as though God dried up my creek bed and now I had to learn to hear through another channel.

Jesus People

When I came out of a traditional church into the Jesus Movement, it was very interesting to watch who accepted whom. Long-haired hippie types were thrown in with the straight types. All were authentic young converts on fire for God. It wasn't just that the conservative types rejected the radical element; many of those long-haired young people were not very receptive to those they considered staid and stuck in traditions. This happens throughout the Church in many ways. And yet, all are Jesus People, carrying Jesus to others.

Those who are versed in the history of the Church realize that God has often spoken through unusual vessels.

Of course, back in the old days it was the norm. But if Jesus showed up in person today, what would He look like? If John the Baptist showed up at our Sunday-morning meeting or midweek Bible luncheon, how would we welcome the scruffy wilderness man with the booming voice? Imagine taking him to Starbucks to share a few honey-dipped locusts around one of those little tables. Soon everyone in the place would know how to repent for his or her sins.

Sooner or later, we learn a simple truth: Our Father God will use someone we would not. It might be a crabby neighbor, an actor on a TV show, an unsaved boss or our two-year-old child. He speaks through them all.

In *Encounters with a Supernatural God*, my wife wrote, "As believers in the one Body of Christ, we all need to learn how to listen to each other. We need to take a step back and let those rise to speak whom God has anointed for specific times and places."[2] Amen. Let it be·so!

Go Wash in the River!

Naaman was the captain of the army, a valiant warrior who served under the leadership of the king of Syria (see 2 Kings 5:1-27). Naaman had a great reputation, except for one major problem—he was a leper. According to 2 Kings 5, Naaman's wife had a servant girl who had come from Israel; she had been captured during a war. The little girl knew of the ministry of the prophet Elisha. Innocently, the servant girl suggested to her mistress that her master, Naaman, go to Samaria to find the prophet Elisha.

Naaman made an appeal to the king of Syria and, surprisingly, he granted the request. The king of Syria sent his greatest warrior, Naaman, off to enemy territory carrying a letter asking that Namaan be healed, along with an offering of 10 talents of silver, 6,000 shekels of gold and 10 changes of clothes. The king of Israel received him, but of course he couldn't help him. Then Naaman went with his horses and his chariots and stood outside the doorway of the house of Elisha. But Elisha did not appear. Instead he sent out a messenger with a "word" about what Naaman was to do. The instructions were, "Go and wash in the Jordan seven times, and your flesh shall be restored to you and you shall be clean" (v. 10). The nature of the response offended Naaman, and he "went away in a rage" (v. 12).

We can all identify with Naaman. Possibly, just possibly, there is a bit of his pride in each of us. We all have preconceived ideas about how God should answer our prayers. We expect God to speak one particular way. He does not, and off we run to throw a pity party. Remember the adage "God offends the mind to reveal the heart."

Naaman's servants wouldn't let him sulk. They sought him out and made an in-your-face appeal to Naaman: "My father, had the prophet told you to do some great thing, would you not have done it? How much more then, when he says to you, 'Wash, and be clean?'" (v. 13).

Naaman must have been going through great inner turmoil. He was a proud man, but humility was being required of him in order to receive healing from the hand of the Lord. Such barriers also may stand in our way of receiving from our King.

To his credit, Naaman did humble himself. He obeyed. He went down and dipped himself seven times in the Jordan according to the word of the man of God; and his flesh was restored like the flesh of a little child, and he was healed. He heard and followed God's word, even when it was delivered by an ordinary servant and involved performing a seemingly meaningless task.

Barriers to Receiving

We each need to grow in the art of hearing His voice through whatever ways and means God chooses. But if we are honest, we realize that we have barriers that need to be identified and removed by His loving hand. The good news is that He is more than willing to help us. Following His lead, our barriers will eventually fall.

For example, I have had "women issues" in my past. But by the grace of God, and the help of my dear wife, many now consider me a champion for women in ministry. (I really had little choice. I could bless what the Father was doing or be left behind!)

Some people seem to be HTRs while others tend to be ETRs. "HTR" stands for "hard to receive" and "ETR" stands for "easy to receive." HTRs—those who find it hard to receive God's word or His transforming help—should not be discouraged. My advice to HTRs: Spend lots of time simply worshiping God. Worship has been a major key the Master has used to transform many hearts. Giant oak trees of stubbornness and fear fall before the transforming love of our Father. Theological backgrounds, traditions, culture, ethnic origins, hurts and wounds of the past can't withstand His light. God is bigger and brighter than all of our issues. When we stand before Him in worship, He has access to our spirits and our souls.

Common obstacles to hearing God's voice:

- Lack of faith
- Lack of a strong commitment to Jesus as Lord
- The presence of sin
- Ignorance of the Scripture
- Lack of quality teaching
- Fear of man and rejection
- Fear of being deceived
- Guilty feelings
- Hurts from the past[3]

Many of these relate to other people. Like Adam and Eve, we hide behind fig leaves. Our fig leaves shield our hearts and souls just as effectively (or ineffectively) from God's approaching presence and thereby from true freedom.[4] They also obstruct our fellowship with others.

We can overcome any and all of the barriers that remain between us and God. There is healing for any ailment that has ever existed. The cure is as old as the universe itself. It is the love of God. Love heals.

How does healing happen? How can we get into the flow of our Father's love so that we can stop hiding from Him and really be able to hear His voice?

Receiving Love Through the Body

The Law reads: "You shall love the Lord your God with all your heart, and with all your soul, and with all your strength, and with all your mind; and your neighbor as yourself" (Luke 10:27). When Jesus came, He didn't change that. He said, "Do this, and you will live" (Luke 10:28). If we want to see the barriers in our heart and soul dissolve, we must ask the Holy Spirit to help us receive the gift of love that proceeds from our brothers and sisters. In a circular fashion, what goes around will come around. We will become a channel of God's love for them too. We will hear God's voice for them and they will hear it for us. Some of what we hear will be wordless—a kind of cleansing stream of healing love. Some of what we will hear will be very specific, and God's words will melt the barriers in our heart, remove the log in our eye and lead us into all truth.

We are to love one another as the Father loved Jesus. The mutual love that exists in the Godhead is our example. The world is waiting to hear a clear sound from the Church. We have been in practice sessions tuning up long enough. Do you want the world to hear the voice of God? His voice is most fully audible when brothers and sisters in Christ love each other.

Together we make up the very Bride of Christ. Being a part of the Bride of Christ is more than just sitting next to someone in a church service or one of our great conference settings. Love has to be practical.

Recently I went through a very difficult battle. It was more than what my family and I could handle on our own. It was a battle with the big C-word—cancer. I had to cancel all my traveling engagements, so we had no income for our ministry team. But thank God for the Body of Christ. My family and I, usually the ones to be giving out love, were on the receiving end. It was a humbling experience—one in which I still hear the voice of God.

The big C of cancer was vanquished by God's multifaceted C: the Community of Christ embraced the Cross with Compassion and Care. Every evening for weeks people brought us meals. Intercessors around the world lifted up prayers on our behalf. Believers enforced the victory of the cross of Christ over the powers of darkness. Encouraging words through emails, cards and people I had never met all merged together into an experience of the love of the Body of Christ. The outcome? The big C became a little *c*, and cancer bowed its knee at the name of Christ Jesus the Lord. Thank God for the Body of Christ and the finished work of the cross.

As we walk in the love of our brothers and sisters, we step out of the old chains that have prevented us from enjoying barrier-free intimacy with God. We will hear God's voice better with each passing year. We will become His mouthpieces to our unsaved loved ones and friends and to our neighborhoods, workplaces, cities and nations.

Guess what? We might even enjoy hearing God through our brothers and sisters.

Think About It

1. Think of the names of your least favorite brothers and sisters in Christ. Some may be family members. You may not be acquainted with others; perhaps you dislike them even though you have only read a book or heard a

news report about them. It would help you hear God's voice if you could appreciate them with God's love, wouldn't it? Ask Him to give you His heart for the people you have named. He will answer your prayer.

2. Can you identify some of your fig leaves, the barriers behind which you hide? Again, can you bring these to your Father, trusting that He will help you with them?

Chapter Eight

Our Need to Discern

And a stranger they simply will not follow, but will flee from
him, because they do not know the voice of strangers.

JOHN 10:5

Do not quench the Spirit; do not despise prophetic utterances.
But examine everything carefully; hold fast to that which is good;
abstain from every form of evil.

1 THESSALONIANS 5:19-22

"And a stranger they simply will not follow" (John 10:5).
This chapter will help that statement become a reality for
you. Let's learn to recognize the voice of God so well that
all the other voices sound unfamiliar.

Let's not be like some people I know (and you proba-
bly know some as well) who would benefit from some lessons in discernment. Instead of making the time to take
driver's training classes, such people quickly get into the
fastest car they can find and go off to the races. Some, sad
to say, end up in a ditch or become casualties of driving
without a license! Let's avoid the ditches. Let's get our per-
mits first, while being mentored by others, and then graduate to driving alone. Where hearing God is concerned,
driver's education includes discernment lessons.

The Need for Discerning of Spirits

The gift of discerning of spirits, which is listed in the New Testament as one of the gifts of the Spirit, is desperately needed in today's Church culture. This gift helps a believer distinguish what motivates spiritual activity. It helps a Christian see through the gray areas and differentiate light from darkness. C. Peter Wagner has defined discerning of spirits as follows:

> The gift of discerning of spirits is the special ability that God gives to certain members of the Body of Christ to know with assurance whether certain behavior purported to be God is in reality divine, human or satanic (see 1 Cor. 12:10; Acts 5:1-11; 16:16-18; 1 John 4:1-6; Matt. 16:21-23).[1]

In *The Beginner's Guide to Spiritual Gifts*, Sam Storms shares some examples of the gift of discerning of spirits in operation:

- Acts 16:16-18, where Paul discerned that the power of a certain slave girl was in fact a demonic spirit.
- Acts 13:8-11, where Paul discerned that Elymas the magician was demonically energized in his attempt to oppose the presentation of the gospel.
- Acts 14:8-10, where again Paul discerned ("saw") that a man had faith to be healed.
- When a person is able to discern whether or not a problem in someone's life is demonic or merely the consequence of other emotional and psycho-

logical factors, or perhaps a complex combination of both.

- When people with this gift are often able to detect or discern the presence of demonic spirits in a room or some such location.
- In Acts 8:20-24, Peter was said to "see" (not physically, but to perceive or sense) that Simon Magus was filled with bitterness and iniquity.
- It would seem that Jesus exercised something along the lines of this gift when he looked at Nathanael and described him as a man "in which is no guile" (John 1:47). In John 2:25 it is said that Jesus "knew what was in man."[2]

Bottom line: This gift helps the believer see below the bottom line!

The Wolf in Sheep's Clothing

When the outward appearance of the wolf is disguised, the human eye cannot immediately discern the wolf. However, the sheepdog will not be deceived, even by the sheep's clothing. He is not deceived because he does not judge by his eyesight but by his sense of smell. The wolf may look like a sheep, but he still smells like a wolf. In Scripture, discernment is like a sense of smell, acting independently of the natural eyesight.

Isaiah the prophet, foreseeing the ministry of Jesus as the Messiah, the anointed one, declares that "the spirit of the LORD . . . shall make him of quick understanding [literally, quick of scent] in the fear of the LORD: and he shall not judge after the sight of his eyes, neither reprove after the hearing of his ears" (Isa. 11:2-3, *KJV*). Those to whom God commits the care of His sheep must likewise, through the Holy Spirit, be quick of scent.

Wisely Judging Revelation

What would you think if you had a spiritual experience that made your hair stand on end? Would you write it off as absolutely satanic or crazy because it didn't fit into your theological grid? Consider some of the experiences of Daniel, Isaiah or Ezekiel recorded in the Old Testament. Daniel lay weary for days because of the impact of a supernatural vision. Isaiah had his lips seared by a burning coal. Ezekiel was forced to lie on his side for 390 days straight. Then there's Zechariah, Paul and John the beloved disciple. An angel strikes Zechariah dumb, Paul is blinded, John sees visions of such magnitude that the entire book of Revelation is inadequate to record them.

We need the gift of discernment, don't we? Most of us in the Western world, if confronted with such events, would tend to chalk them up to psychological disturbances or the devil. Entire segments of the Body of Christ have written off hearing from the Lord because of fears about being deceived and led astray. It's true that such experiences can come from the supernatural power of the enemy, from the human mind or from God Himself. Yet, as we have seen in this book, God wants us to recognize His voice, and our Master is very capable of preserving us from harm and deception.

Jesus said:

For everyone who asks, receives; and he who seeks, finds; and to him who knocks, it shall be opened. Now suppose one of you fathers is asked by his son for a fish; he will not give him a snake instead of a fish, will he? How much more shall your heavenly Father give the Holy Spirit to those who ask Him? (Luke 11:10,13).

We can trust our Father. If we ask Him for the things of the Holy Spirit in the name of Christ, we will get the real things, not counterfeits. Two of His best gifts are wisdom and discernment. We need to stick close to Jesus and ask God to enable us to grow in them!

Sources of Revelation

The Scriptures teach us that spiritual revelation or communication comes from one of three sources: the Holy Spirit, the human soul or the realm of evil spirits.

The *Holy Spirit* is the only true source of pure revelation. It was the Holy Spirit who moved the prophets of the Old Testament and the witnesses of the New Testament. "No [true] prophecy was ever made by an act of human will, but men moved by the Holy Spirit spoke from God" (2 Pet. 1:21). The Greek word for "moved," *phero*, means "to be borne along or even to be driven along as a wind."

Thoughts, ideas and inspirations that don't originate with the Holy Spirit can be voiced by the *human soul*—the second source. These come out of our unsanctified portion of our emotions (see Jer. 23:16 and Ezek. 13:1-6). As Ezekiel the prophet said, these are prophecies out of men's own hearts. He reports the words of God as he heard them, "Woe to the foolish prophets who are following their own spirit and have seen nothing" (Ezek. 13:3).

The third source of revelation, *evil spirits*, can appear to be angels of light (good voices), but they always speak lies because they serve the chief liar and father of lies, Satan. Messages delivered through evil spirits are often especially dangerous to people ignorant of God's Word or inexperienced in discernment because Satan loves to mix just enough truth with his lies to trick gullible people.

Remember the slave girl with a spirit of divination described in Acts 16? She spoke the truth about the disciples, but she got her information from a satanic source. Eventually, the apostle Paul had heard enough: He was irritated (something just didn't seem right!), and he commanded the spirit of divination to leave her. He discerned that her accurate revelations were coming from the wrong supernatural source. When the slave girl's owners became upset because their extra income had disappeared along with the evil spirit, Paul's discernment was confirmed. After all, God's servants don't sell their services as psychics.

Testing Revelation

The only way we can accurately and safely approach interpreting the motivation behind revelatory activity of any kind is to ask God for the spirit of wisdom and understanding. As reviewed in chapter 3, God still speaks today through many different avenues, including visions, dreams, His inner voice, His external audible voice, His creation, and so forth. Yet our most important source of revelation is the canon of Scripture. Since the Bible is our absolute standard against which we must test spiritual experiences, let's look at nine scriptural tests.

To be assured of receiving accurate and valid revelation, we can apply the following list of nine scriptural tests.

1. *Does the revelation edify, exhort or console?* "But one who prophesies speaks to men for edification and exhortation and consolation" (1 Cor. 14:3). The end purpose of all true revelation is to build up, admonish and encourage the people of God. It is summed up best in 1 Cor. 14:26: "Let all things be done for edification."

2. *Is it in agreement with God's Word?* "All Scripture is given by inspiration of God" (2 Tim. 3:16, *NKJV*). Where the Holy Spirit has said "yea and amen" in Scripture, He also says yea and amen in revelation. He never contradicts Himself.

3. *Does it exalt Jesus Christ?* "He shall glorify Me; for He shall take of Mine, and shall disclose it to you" (John 16:14). All true revelation centers on the person of Jesus Christ and exalts Him (see Rev. 19:10).

4. *Does it have good fruit?* "Beware of the false prophets, who come to you in sheep's clothing, but inwardly are ravenous wolves. You will know them by their fruits" (Matt. 7:15-16).

The true voice of God will produce fruit in character and conduct that agrees with the fruit of the Holy Spirit (see Gal. 5:22-23 and Eph. 5:9).

5. *If it predicts a future event, does it come to pass?* "When a prophet speaks in the name of the LORD, if the thing does not come about or come true, that is the thing which the LORD has not spoken. The prophet has spoken it presumptuously; you shall not be afraid of him" (Deut. 18: 22).

6. *Does the revelatory turn people toward God or away from Him?* (See Deut. 13:1-5.) If a person's words seem to be accurate, but they end up turning people away from following Jesus Christ as the Son of God, then it is a mistake to adhere to his or her ministry.

7. *Does it produce liberty or bondage?* "For you have not received a spirit of slavery leading to fear again, but you have received a spirit of adoption as sons by which we cry out, 'Abba! Father!'" (Rom. 8:15). True revelation given by the Holy Spirit produces liberty, not bondage (see 1 Cor. 14:33 and 2 Tim. 1:7).

8. *Does it produce life or death?* "For the letter kills, but the Spirit gives life" (2 Cor. 3:6). The authentic voice of God always produces growth and

life-giving energy, not hopelessness, stagna-
tion or defeat.

9. *Does the Holy Spirit bear witness that it is true?* "And
   as for you, the anointing which you received
   from Him abides in you, and you have no need
   for anyone to teach you; but as His anointing
   teaches you about all things, and is true and is
   not a lie, and just as it has taught you, you
   abide in Him" (1 John 2:27). The Holy Spirit
   is called "the Spirit of truth" (John 16:13). His
   indwelling presence in our hearts and minds
   provides us with a kind of supernatural common sense about the accuracy of words that
   seem to be from God. This ninth test is the
   most subjective and therefore must be used in
   conjunction with the previous eight standards.[3]

May God give us the ability to walk in the grace of discerning His voice from all the "voices of strangers." May
we each experience the fullness of the spirit of wisdom
and revelation in the knowledge of our Lord Jesus Christ
(see Eph. 1:17-19). Let's pause to lift a prayer for His help:

*Father God, Your Word tells me to not despise
prophesying, to test all things and to hold fast to what is
good. Teach me to discern Your voice. I lift up Your Word as
my standard. Help me to be a wise steward of Your grace,
dear Lord. Teach me to discern good from evil. Grant me an
appropriate fear of You and the wisdom to judge revelation
properly. In Jesus' mighty name, amen.*

Think About It

1. Read Acts 10, the story of Peter and Cornelius.
    Apply the nine scriptural tests to Peter's vision.
    Does his experience pass the tests?

2. Wisdom (which helps us know what to do next)
    goes hand in hand with discernment (which
    helps us know the source of what we observe).
    Are you stronger in one of these qualities than
    in the other? Are you lacking in one or both of
    them? Do you have trusted friends who can
    help you compensate for your relative weak-
    ness by giving wise counsel or by confirming
    your own discernment?

Chapter Nine

Our Geiger Counter of Guidance

Although the Lord has given you the bread of privation and water of oppression, He, your Teacher, will no longer hide Himself, but your eyes will behold your Teacher. And your ears will hear a word behind you, "This is the way, walk in it," whenever you turn to the right or to the left.

ISAIAH 30:20-21

Do you remember playing the Hot or Cold game as a child? You would be blindfolded and some object in the room would be selected by the others for you to try to find, blindly groping around the room. Your playmates would shout, "You're getting warmer. Naw, you're *cold*. Warm, warmer, HOT!" Of course, "hot" meant you were getting closer to the desired object, and "cold" meant you were going in the wrong direction.

The Geiger counter works a little bit like that game. It's an interesting instrument, named for Hans Geiger, the German physicist who invented it in 1928. The Geiger counter can detect the presence and intensity of radiation (the spontaneous emission of energy from radioactive elements, most notably uranium) by using a gas-filled tube that briefly conducts electricity when radiation makes the gas conductive. The Geiger counter amplifies this signal into a series of clicks. The closer it gets to the radioactive substance and the greater the intensity of the substance's radiation, the louder and faster the clicking noise becomes.

I have often thought this is a lot like our approach to hearing God's voice. Our spirit is like the Geiger counter that tells us whether we are closer or farther away. It helps us put all the pieces together. We learn to pay attention to an inner witness. We check in with the Holy Spirit, we listen to our "knower," and our spirit either bears witness, or it doesn't. When we are filled with the Holy Spirit, we have a divine guidance system that comes as part of the package.

Are you getting warmer—closer to what God wants to say? Or are you getting colder—farther away from it? Do pay attention to the signals.

Ten Principles of Divine Guidance

Determining God's will is more an art form than a science. Yet there are basic principles of which we each need to be aware. They are some of the signals that will help us zero in on God's word. Some of the principles in this chapter will be a bit of a review and some of them fresh and new. Let these 10 principles of divine guidance help you hear God's voice, determine His guidance and, most of all, grow closer to God Himself.

1. The Will of God Is Made Known in the Word of God

Some people start trying to listen to the subjective without being grounded first in the objective. They don't have a gauge to judge what they're sensing, hearing, feeling, thinking, or what I call knowings. Here's a very basic example: One day we read in Exodus 20:14, "You shall not commit adultery." That registers in our spirit and stays there. Not long afterward, we are walking in the mall and we see a very attractive person of the opposite sex. Some inner voice suggests something like *Look over there at that good-looking person. Wow!* But because the Scripture is hidden in our heart, it is easy to turn away from that thought. We don't even have to evaluate whether that tempting voice is God's; we know it isn't. The Word (the objective logos) is hidden in our heart, and it informs us that this stray thought should be ignored, that it is in fact the beginning of a temptation. In all guidance, God's Word is the final judge.

2. The Will of God Is Confirmed Through Circumstances

During my senior year of college, I was quite zealous for the Lord. I read a tract on expelling demons and went and did it that day. It worked! Although earlier I had given myself much more to my studies, I had become a full-blown Jesus nut, and I cared little about the pursuit of academic credentials. I was ready to quit college at the end of my first trimester of my senior year, although I needed only 20 more hours to complete my degree.

My grades were still good, but they weren't as high as they once had been. I thought I was ready for full-time ministry. I prayed something like this:

O God, I just want to forget this stuff and get on with my real calling! . . . but if You want me to finish out this year, I ask You to do something. Show me Your will!

Then a surprising thing happened. Even though I was ready to quit in November, with only six months to go until graduation, somehow I received a scholarship for which I hadn't even applied. It was a religious leadership scholarship to help me financially so that I could complete the rest of my year at a secular university. So I decided, *That's a pretty good circumstantial sign. God has answered. I'd better go ahead and complete what I have started!*

I'm glad I completed that degree. I might not have met my wife if I hadn't!

Circumstances alone don't constitute divine guidance, but they can often confirm God's will.

3. The Holy Spirit Speaks from Where He Dwells

Where does God dwell? Not only does He dwell in heaven, but He also dwells within us if we are children of God and we've been filled with the Holy Spirit. According to 1 Corinthians 6:19, "Your body is a temple of the Holy Spirit who is in you." Colossians 1:27 confirms, "Christ in you, the hope of glory." He speaks to us from where He dwells.

Have you listened to your heart lately? What is beating in your heart? John 16:13 states, "But when He, the Spirit of truth, comes, He will guide you into all the truth; for He will not speak on His own initiative, but whatever He hears, He will speak; and He will disclose to you what is to come." The Holy Spirit is heaven's representative in all-true guidance.

4. Divine Guidance Comes from Meeting God's Conditions

What are the divine conditions that must be met for guidance to be unlocked? Has he heard our cry? If we meet His conditions, He will surely guide us.

Read Isaiah 58, where we find some of God's requirements described. The chapter speaks about honoring God
and caring for the downtrodden, observing the Sabbath
and not pointing the finger in accusation of others. Above
all, we see that having a humble heart is of the utmost
importance.

If our attitude toward God and our fellow human
beings is not arrogant, then God's corresponding promise
is "And the LORD will continually guide you" (Isa. 58:11).
The conditions are listed first.

5. Peace of God Accompanies True Guidance

Peace does not mean there is no storm. Peace does not
mean there's no warfare either. God's peace creates a center of quiet in the midst of turbulence. True guidance
from God does not push us; it brings peace and satisfaction. James remarks, "The wisdom from above is first
pure, then peaceable, gentle, reasonable, full of mercy and
good fruits, unwavering, without hypocrisy" (Jas. 3:17).

Notice that James states that the wisdom of God is
"unwavering." That's an interesting interjection. It means
God doesn't say one thing one day and something totally
different the next. The Holy Spirit's guidance is constant
and unwavering. It can be tested by time and tested by content. God's guidance is not nervous or tentative. God is not
the author of confusion but of steadfastness and peace.

6. Much Guidance from God Comes Unnoticed

Much of our guidance comes undetected. We're often
unaware that we are being guided. This is because we've

asked Him to continually guide us. We want to do His will. It's also because of the sovereignty of God. God wants us to do His will more than we want to do it. He is quietly releasing His thoughts into our sanctified minds so that we can make wise decisions.

Humility is the key that unlocks God's provision: "He leads the humble in justice, and He teaches the humble His way" (Ps. 25:9).

> *Thank You, Lord, for Your gentle nudges, whispers in the night and occasional pushes and shoves. Thank You for guiding us even when we cannot tell that it is You.*

7. Divine Guidance Does Not Mean We Know All the Details

Of course, that may not be what we want to hear. We prefer to be able to know everything, don't we?

Each of us is like a child who wants to see a great parade that is coming down the street, only there's a tall fence separating the child from the parade. The child isn't tall enough to see over the fence. He or she can hear the sound of something coming. It sounds exciting and the child wants to see it. The child gets excited, then frustrated, but suddenly he or she finds there's a little knothole in the fence. Now as the child is looking through the knothole, the parade is passing by and he or she spots a funny clown. The child is so excited, "Oh, I just love this parade; this is just wonderful."

Only the next time the child takes a peek, he or she doesn't see anything. Why? Well, it's only a gap between the parade events. The child says, "I think it's all over." But it isn't over at all; it's just a pause.

The child can still hear the music, so he or she takes another look. But this time there's a new problem. Somebody's standing in the way. The child may stomp his or her feet and throw a fit, or the child may decide to poke a stick through the hole and say, "Hey, you. Move!" We could say the child has issues of character development and that he or she is learning patience.

Now the child turns and something else catches his or her attention—a ladder going up the side of the house. The child scrambles up the ladder to the top of the roof. From the rooftop view, the child can see the beginning, the middle and all the way to the end of the parade.

It's the same with God's guidance. We want the rooftop view. The Lord wants us, in a sense, to have the rooftop view we so much desire. But most of the time, we only get to look through the knotholes in the fence. There may be a special time when we see A, B, C and even a portion of X, Y and Z. Those awesome experiences can ruin us for life (in a good way).

But most of the time, we will only see what is in front of us. That's just the way it is. It keeps us reliant on God and humble. Just the same, we can enjoy the parade.

8. The Process of Guidance Is Not Always Pleasant

In Isaiah 55:8-9, God declares:

> "My thoughts are not your thoughts, neither are your ways My ways," declares the LORD. "For as the heavens are higher than the earth, so are My ways higher than your ways, and My thoughts than your thoughts."

The New Testament teaches us that we can have the "mind of Christ" (1 Cor. 2:16). But there is a noticeable gap between our own thoughts, opinions, reasoning and traditions, and His. We are unaccustomed to His ways. We think He should do things in a certain order, and He seems to like to mess that up. God's guidance might not seem to be very pleasant, because we experience heartbreak and disappointment.

If we choose His way over our way, it might seem painful for the moment, but the end result will be good.

9. Hearing God Speak Should Prompt Us to Action

God's Word is compelling. If we act on it, we'll hear more. In Daniel 11:32 we read, "But the people who know their God will display strength and take action."

I've noted this principle earlier. Many times people are looking for the next word from God. The word for them today is "Have you done the last thing? What was the last thing God said to you to do? Have you completed it?"

Don't be overcome by a sense of failure. Ask God for another chance. I've been learning our God is the God of the *fiftieth* chance, not only the second chance. His mercies are new every morning. Do learn from the past, but forget what lies behind and press forward into the upward call of Christ Jesus.

10. Guidance Is a Skill to Be Learned over a Lifetime

If we have heard God speak once, we cannot assume we've learned how to hear Him once and for all. We are on a lifetime walk with Him.

I learned early on that I can hear the Holy Spirit's voice for other people. It is a great privilege and responsibility to be gifted in such a manner. But when it comes to getting guidance for myself, I can't seem to hear Him as clearly. I hear Him the same way others hear Him for themselves, through my relationship with Him.

I should cultivate the gifts of the Holy Spirit so that God can use me to release blessings to others. But to really grow in the very subjective art of hearing God for myself, I need to be like John the beloved and lean my head upon the chest of my Messiah and Master, listening for the very heartbeat of God. You and I need to cultivate a friendship with Jesus. Then we will be able to hear God in all His multifaceted modes of expression. We will find that true guidance is not just a one-time thing. Hearing the voice of God depends on having a lifetime relationship, and that can never be taken away. It is walking with the Guide Himself.

As we review God's principles and grow in loving Him, our internal Geiger counter will become more and more reliable. It will guide us to the source of power, even when the light seems dim and it's hard to find the way. Yes, we are each given a Geiger counter of guidance. We just need to learn to turn it on and use it.

Think About It

1. Choose 1 of the 10 principles of divine guid-
    ance and tell somebody how it has worked for
    you. If you don't have someone to tell, write
    down your thoughts about how you relied on
    the principle.

2. With informed hindsight, reflect on a circum-
    stance in your life that illustrates principle 6,
    Much Guidance from God Comes Unnoticed.
    What guidance has come that you acknowl-
    edge now, but which you did not recognize at
    the moment?

Chapter Ten

Our Journey's End

Thou hast taken account of my wanderings; put my tears in Thy bottle; are they not in Thy book? Then my enemies will turn back in the day when I call; this I know, that God is for me.

PSALM 56:8-9

Not that I have already obtained it, or have already become perfect, but I press on in order that I may lay hold of that for which also I was laid hold of by Christ Jesus. Brethren, I do not regard myself as having laid hold of it yet; but one thing I do: forgetting what lies behind and reaching forward to what lies ahead, I press on toward the goal for the prize of the upward call of God in Christ Jesus.

PHILIPPIANS 3:12-14

I have fought the good fight, I have finished the course, I have kept the faith.

2 TIMOTHY 4:7

God chooses each one of us to fulfill a distinct purpose and destiny in Him. His call causes us to cast away the "fishing nets" of the things that are familiar to us to become pilgrims on a journey. Like Jesus' first disciples, we don't know what the future holds. Christ helps us

to be determined, no matter the cost, to run hard to follow Him in order to fulfill His will. We struggle at times
and we get frustrated, tempted to throw in the towel,
but we continue. The once-bright pathway disappears.
We thought we had heard our Master say where we were
headed. Yet by sight we appear no further down the road
than when we first began.

Learning from the lessons of believers who have gone
before us, we realize that all progress in the Christian life
comes by faith. We turn to our road map over and over
again. We lean our ear in His direction to receive encouragement for today. Yes, it may be an arduous path, but it
is indeed an adventure. We must proceed. The requirements: hearing God's voice and obeying it.

Has God Said?

The enemy attempts his same old tricks one after another.
How often have we heard God speak clearly, only to have
it followed by the devil's sly comeback, "Has God *really*
said?"—which is the same question the serpent asked
Eve in the Garden. The enemy has repeated those words
in the ear of every person who has ever tried to follow the
Lord God.

Undermining the Word of the Lord is one of the enemy's main ploys. Unless we have God's Word rooted
deeply inside, we can easily get off the track because of
Satan's insinuations. Vaguely trying to quote God's Word,
we repeat Eve's mistake. "Don't eat—in fact, don't even
touch it!" (Eve added the last phrase, "don't even touch it"
[see Gen. 3:3]. God hadn't forbidden touching the fruit.)

Like Eve, we misquote God, and we are caught off balance. Proverbs 30:5-6 warns us, "Every word of God is tested; He is a shield to those who take refuge in Him. Do not add to His words lest He reprove you, and you be proved a liar."

Many of us struggle to know whether we actually heard God. But that was not the case with Adam and Eve. There was no doubt that God had spoken to them. So the serpent's strategy bypassed the question of whether God had spoken; he questioned God's intent. The enemy knows the Word rather well, so he distorts it subtly, a little here and there, without our even realizing it. It will happen to you: When the devil can't stop you from hearing God's word, He moves on to another strategy of distorting the goodness of God Himself.

I wish Eve had stood firm: "Yes, that's what God said! God is good, and He knows what I need. I'm not going to listen to snakes!" Now I am not an Eve-basher, I just want us to learn all we can in order to avoid similar pitfalls. Remember, Isaiah said, "All we like sheep have gone astray; we have turned, every one, to his own way" (Isa. 53:6, *NKJV*).

Line of Fire

Sometimes we feel as though we are the direct target of spiritual warfare. It's because we are ambassadors of One who has vanquished all the collective forces of the dark side. We may not be the direct target, but we may be the most visible one.

Therefore, like Jesus our Messiah in the garden of Gethsemane, we kneel before our Lord and maker, and we receive grace and strength for the battle. Putting on the full armor of God, we arm ourselves for the fight. Challenges, doubts, fears and questions come at us from multiple directions. Taking up the shield of faith, we extinguish the fiery darts of the evil one. Standing confident in His spoken and confirmed word, we wage war against the spirits of wickedness and deception. Submitted to God, we resist the devil, who must flee from us. We rise with the high praises of God in our mouths, driving the deceiver farther away with our worship.

We hear the voice of God. The enemy tries to snatch the word away. We hang on to it. Somewhere in there, we begin to realize that maybe God's goal is something more than giving us another word. Have you ever felt like the Word got a hold of you? He is the Living Word.

Tested by the Word

"The words of the LORD are pure words; as silver tried in a furnace on the earth, refined seven times" (Ps. 12:6).

Often, when we receive an exciting revelation from God, He uses the revelation itself to test us and purify us so that our character will be able to convey the word to others. I wonder how Joseph felt as he endured trials and testing, pits and prisons, because of his two life-shaping dreams. It took many years for him to see the fulfillment of those words.

I wonder how Abram felt when the Lord told him to move from his familiar surroundings to a strange land. Would he listen and obey, leave his country and follow Yahweh? If so, God said He would bless him with a lineage as numerous as the stars of the sky. Years of testing transpired, as Abraham believed God. He had to be convinced that the voice that had spoken to him was not a crazy notion in his head.

I imagine that his first step of obedience, packing up and moving to Haran, was the hardest one of all. When he took that first step, believing he had heard God, he found that taking another step would not be so hard. Eventually his trail of hearing and obeying brought him to the land of promise, only to find the land suffering from severe famine.

Along the way, his failures reflected his capitulation to Satan's ploys, but they didn't disqualify him. He attempted to produce an heir through Hagar, trying to fulfill God's word in his own strength and understanding. All the trials prepared Abraham for his ultimate test of faith (see Gen. 22)—being asked to sacrifice his own miraculously conceived son, the son of his old age. Abraham, by now a giant in faith, believed that if need be, God would raise his son Isaac up from the dead to fulfill his promise!

These trials were all a part of the necessary steps of faith that Abraham needed to take. Many years later, he saw God's promises fulfilled, with accompanying struggles, trials, testing—and a refining of God's word.

All through the Bible we see the long journeys of those who heard from Him in one radical way or another. Consider Moses. How many seemingly endless years did he faithfully follow God's voice?

The little shepherd boy David—how many years after he received his word from God did he become king? How many times was he tested by the question, Did God really say that? How many times did he wonder if Samuel had been right? How many times was he pressured by his own men to fulfill God's word by his own strength?

Each had received a promise, but when the testing of those words came, each of those men of God responded differently to God's words and to the subsequent testings. All of them failed along the way. But God used their failures as part of their character development process. Even failures can be used to help keep His word pure.

What Will Our Response Be?

Should we be exceptions to this pattern? If we can hear God's voice and have been called to even a small task in building His kingdom, let's rejoice that we have been found worthy to be called God's children and to be tested on the very promises He gives to us.

God will not allow us to be tested beyond what we can bear (see 1 Cor. 10:13). He's a loving Father who wants to see His children succeed. He simply allows trials in our life so that we will have the proven character needed to carry the message. "We also exult in our tribulations, knowing that tribulation brings about perseverance; and perseverance, proven character; and proven character, hope; and hope does not disappoint" (Rom. 5:3-5).

He tests His very words on purpose so that we will reach our hand heavenward to grasp His hand of mercy and grace. He is a good Father. He wants us to grow up and to be as much like His Son as we can be. Although we may find it difficult to comprehend His mysterious ways, we can be sure of *His* character, which is good through and through.

How many times have I allowed God's word to slip away because I thought the testings were simply evidence that I had heard it wrong? How many times did I lose out when the little voice said, *Did God* really *say that?*

Ministry to the Nations

Years ago, I was the pastor of a small congregation in a college town in Missouri. I was dedicated to my flock but restless on the inside. Healing evangelist Mahesh Chavda came to minister to our congregation, and at the end of the service, I felt an urge to go and pull on his coattails as if I were drawing forth an anointing from him. I took hold of his suit jacket. A strong current of God's power overwhelmed me. The next thing I knew, I was lying on the platform!

Lying there under the power of God, I began to see a vision. I could see a man's hand with a globe rotating in it. A sort of ticker tape with words on it came before my sight, listing the names of nation after nation. I could read the list of nations clearly as they rushed before my mind: Guatemala, Haiti, Israel—on and on. I was stunned and wondered what all this meant. At that point in my life, I had only been outside of the United States one time.

Then a word came to me, "You cannot perceive and receive this in your natural mind; because in your natural mind there is self-doubt. You can only perceive and receive this in your spirit through faith." The Holy Spirit continued to hover over me, and a second time I saw the same vision. A globe was turning in a man's hand with names of nations circulating before my eyes. I began to analyze what was happening, skeptical that it could be from God. The voice came to me a second time, clearly whispering the exact same words, convicting my heart as the words settled deep down inside of me: "You cannot perceive and receive this in your natural mind; because in your natural mind there is self-doubt. You can only perceive and receive this in your spirit through faith."

I tried to get up but was unsuccessful. It was as if the Holy Spirit had set a rock on my chest to make sure that I could not move until I got the picture. The vision occurred a third time: a globe revolving in a man's hand with the list of the nations. By now, the names of the nations were burning in my heart.

As the words began to settle deep within me, something more transpired. Faith was awakened inside of me. God spoke other things to me as I lay there—promises from His throne and conditions that had to be met. Finally, His presence began to lift from me. I sat up. I was dazed. I arose. I was changed, and I believed what God had promised. I had very little understanding of what this meant, the cost it would entail or any other details. But I knew that I knew that I knew—that I was born for a ministry to the nations.

I learned years ago to kneel on the promises. That means I pray such promises back into the Father's hearing. It brings such words to life to pray them into being!

By the grace of God, I have now ministered in every one of the nations revealed to me that day—about 30 in all. God told me that He would give to me the blessing of John Wesley—"that the world would be my parish." It has been so.

I can't spell out all the second-guessing I have been through, the sleepless nights, the wrestling against the demonic hosts, the cost of leaving family and friends to move to another state just because He said so, the loneliness of leaving my family behind to go out and do the Master's call.

Michal Ann and I have had to pick up our cross many times to walk out that word and others. We feel we are in good company, following in others' footsteps.

It's worth the price—to hear His voice, to know His kiss, to sense His touch! Satisfaction does not come as much through finishing a task as it does through increased intimacy with Him. He is my journey's beginning—and its end.

This Is My Father's World

As I penned these words, my entire being was once again overwhelmed with God's presence. I had just come back in from my southern-facing front porch, which overlooks the beautiful hills of Franklin, Tennessee. The sun was setting and the sky was ignited with a display of heavenly colors. In gratitude to God, I lifted my glass and gave God a toast: "To the promises of God and to the God who promises!"

With tears of gratitude, I then sang this old hymn to Him. Read these words and sing them if you know the tune.

> This is my Father's world, and to my listening ears
> All nature sings, and round me rings the music of
>   the spheres.
> This is my Father's world: I rest me in the thought
> Of rocks and trees, of skies and seas;
>   His hand the wonders wrought.

This is my Father's world, the birds their carols raise,
The morning light, the lily white, declare their
    Maker's praise.
This is my Father's world: He shines in all that's fair;
In the rustling grass I hear him pass;
    He speaks to me everywhere.
This is my Father's world, O let me ne'er forget
That though the wrong seems oft so strong, God
    is the ruler yet.
This is my Father's world, why should my heart
    be sad?
The Lord is King: let the heavens ring! God reigns:
    let the earth be glad![1]

Do you hear Him speaking now to you? He's waiting
to have a moment just with you. Lean your head a bit and
you will hear more than words. You will hear the sound of
love beating in His heart. He is your journey's end. Knowing God is what hearing God is ultimately all about!

Morning by morning he wakens me and opens my
understanding to his will. The Sovereign LORD has
spoken to me, and I have listened (Isa. 50:4, *NLT*).

Do you hear what I hear?

Study Guide

The following study guide will help you develop the ability to discern and listen to God's voice. Scripture passages, excerpts from the book and reflection questions have been designed to help you develop a deeper relationship with your heavenly Father. You can use the guide individually, with a friend or in a small group.

If you are studying *The Beginner's Guide to Hearing God* on your own or with a partner, consider starting a "God diary" in which you work through each chapter's reflection questions and write down the ways God is speaking to you. Even if you do not have a partner for the study, find someone—a close friend or your spouse, for instance—to share your thoughts and feelings with as you progress. Writing and then talking about the growth you experience will strengthen you to move forward with confidence.

If you desire to discuss *The Beginner's Guide to Hearing God* within a small group, the following guidelines will maximize your time with each other. In anticipation of your weekly meeting, be sure everyone has a copy of the book. Encourage group members to read the chapter that will be discussed at the meeting, and to write down questions or comments that come to them during the week. Bring your Bible to each study and invite group members to do the same. Each week, the group will practice listening for God's voice and the Bible will be the primary text to help them discern what God might be saying.

During the week, pray that the Holy Spirit will speak to each member of the group. In addition, pray that you will remain sensitive to how God is speaking when the group comes together. When you meet, open each session with prayer, asking the Holy Spirit to come and make His presence and voice known.

After prayer, ask each person to share his or her first impressions of the chapter. As the weeks progress, also take time to let each person share how he or she is learning to discern God's voice. Work through the study guide together, and when you come across a question, encourage each group member to participate.

Finally, try to create an atmosphere that fosters trust within the group and freedom to practice hearing God's voice.

Chapter One:

Our Need to Hear God
Beginning the Adventure

As you were being formed in your mother's womb, a tremendous bond developed between you and your mother. When your brain began to take shape, you started to identify with her voice and her motions. For many, the voice of their mother is the sound of security and love. For others who might have been unexpectedly separated from their mother, there is a deep longing to be connected to the one who cradled them in the womb.

Because we have all been separated from the One who formed us, we also have an inner longing to know the voice of our Creator. In the opening chapter, the author writes:

> *He didn't make us to be mechanical robots that just march around doing preordained things. Our Father God created us to have fellowship with Him. It is our birthright to have an actual relationship with our God* (p. 13).

· Think of two words that describe your relationship with God right now. Why are these words significant?

· How has that relationship changed and developed from when you were a child?

· The author describes the daily relationship that Adam and Eve shared with God in the garden. Read about that in Genesis 2:15-25, and then think of two words that characterize that relationship.

· Have you ever heard God's voice? What did it sound like? In what ways have you experienced His voice?

Most likely, you've struggled to know and hear the voice of God. You've struggled because we have been separated from God. Original sin infected everyone. Consider these words from chapter one:

> *Jesus came to restore humankind into the sweet fellowship that Adam and Eve first had known in the Garden. Sin cut them off from God and they could no longer be*

close to God. Sin in the same way cuts off each of us from God. But sin doesn't have the final word. Because of the cross and the shed blood of Christ Jesus, we can be restored to fellowship. One of the main reasons Jesus came was to enable us to walk in restored communion with God (p. 14).

If you have never asked Jesus to come into your life and to forgive your sins, that's the first step toward hearing God's voice. In Revelation 3, we read that Jesus is standing at the door and knocking—all you need to do is open the door and ask Him into your heart. As you begin this study, ask Jesus to forgive your sins and to come and live with you.

If you feel like you have known Jesus but have been ignoring Him lately, take time to talk with Him right now to reconnect with your Lord and Savior.

If you are with a partner or in a group, take time to confess and express forgiveness of sins to each other through the blood of Jesus.

As you develop a relationship with Jesus, you'll find that you'll want to know more and more of Him.

True fellowship requires that both parties speak and listen, both sharing their hearts deeply with one another. This is the key to keeping all relationships fresh and alive. In an atmosphere of trust, we share our heart with someone else. Communion with God is much more than a ritual or an "information time." It's Spirit-to-spirit time! (p. 15).

Perhaps, like the author, you've had many one-sided conversations with God. James's life changed when he had an experience with a group of people who introduced Him to the Holy Spirit. This powerful experience gave his life a "quantum leap."

• Have you ever had an experience with the Holy Spirit? If so, what was it like?

If we are satisfied and content with the status quo of our spiritual lives, we will never try very hard to hear God's voice. But when we're desperate for guidance or for reassurance, we'll hasten to consult Him.

• How desperate are you to hear God's voice? Are you completely satisfied with your present life, or do you feel that you would do just about anything to hear from Him?

Learning from Fellow Students

When someone begins a new sport, one way they develop their skills and enthusiasm is by watching experienced players. As they see others, a vision forms for who they want to be. The same is true in our walk with God. In this chapter, we read how Abraham became "our finest example of believing God and obeying His voice."

God's Story gives many examples of people who developed a spirit-to-Spirit conversation with God. Read the following passages and reflect on the questions provided.

• Read Genesis 22:1-18. What do you learn about listening to the voice of God from this example of Abraham's life?

- Read Exodus 3. How would you describe Moses' conversation with God?

- Read Luke 1:26-38. How did Mary respond to the voice of God?

Are you ready to begin the adventure of developing your relationship with Your Father?

> *You don't have to wait any longer—classes start every day! School is in session at all times! You can enroll right now and be a student with me in the School of the Spirit where we learn to hear the voice of God* (p. 23).

If you are ready to join in, pray the prayer on pages 23-24.

Chapter Two:

Our Personal Tutor
The School of the Spirit

For children who live in an orphanage, Christmas is a very special time of year. Generous people from all over the world open their hearts to those in need. But after Christmas, many children are soon forgotten—until next year, when they'll receive another gift.

What orphaned children need and long for is the gift of adoption. Any particular gift pales in comparison to the loving presence of a parent. When a child is adopted, she discovers a parent who gives countless gifts throughout the year.

It's the same in the kingdom of God. As an adopted son or daughter, God does not simply want to give us things every once in a while—He wants us to experience His gifts all the time. James Goll writes:

> Father and Son have sent their best to us by giving each of us disciples one very special gift, a gift that keeps giving us more gifts. Would could that be? It's our Comforter, our Guide, the One called alongside to help us out—the Holy Spirit (p. 26).

- What are your impressions of the Holy Spirit? Consider all the different images and impressions you have of Him.

This chapter describes how the Holy Spirit serves as a personal tutor in God's school. After the author had his first powerful experience with the Holy Spirit, he wanted to know more of God. His spirit longed for deeper communication with God's Spirit. Do you want to know your Papa in a deeper way? Consider this advice:

> To get close to Him, you may have to push through misconceptions, spiritual warfare, debates about religious theories and a bunch of plain old opposition, until you come to the place where you and He are rightly related with one another and on good speaking terms (p. 27).

- What types of opposition have you experienced or seen others experience that keep them from knowing intimacy with the Holy Spirit?

- Read John 16:5-16. How do these words of Jesus combat some of that opposition?

- If the Holy Spirit were your personal counselor or tutor, what difference would that make in your life?

Have you entered into the Spirit-filled life? If not, stop everything and throw yourself into your Savior's arms. Tell Him you want to be entirely His. Ask Him for the gift of His Holy Spirit. Enjoy the blessing and power of prayer in asking for the Holy Spirit's presence to come to you right now.

Time to Study the Curriculum

The author describes the amazing variety of classes offered in God's School of the Spirit. Over the past 2,000 years, many Christians just like you have taken these classes and put their knowledge into action. Do you want to take advantage of God's best for you? Below are just a few of those courses. Read the different course descriptions and answer the questions.

- *Holiness 101:* Read John 16:8-11. What are you going to learn in this class? How will that impact your life or the life of others in the world?

- *Holiness 102:* Read Acts 2:1-13. What does the fire of the Spirit empower the disciples to do? What impact does that have on the world?

- *Victorious Living 201:* Read 1 Corinthians 10:6-13. How does God give you a "way out" when you are tempted to give up or sin? If you experienced victory every day in the Spirit, what impact would that have in your life?

- *Victorious Living 202:* Read Galatians 5:16-26. If you were to "live by the Spirit," what fruit would be different in your life? How would that affect those who are close to you?

- *The Future Revealed 101:* Read Acts 16:6-10. How did God reveal the future to Paul? What was God's purpose in giving Paul this vision?

You have a lifetime to experience the power and presence of the Holy Spirit as you study God's Word and get to know Him personally. God wants to do great things in you and through you. He has many gifts waiting for you to open as you say, "Yes, I'll take that course!"

- Read 1 Corinthians 12:1-11 and write down as many other courses you think might be possible in the School of the Spirit.

Time to Get Started

An old Chinese proverb says, "The best time to plant a tree is 20 years ago. The second best time is right now."

No matter where you've been in your Christian life up to this point, it's always the right time to know more of God. If you've been a Christian for 1 day or 40 years, you can always go deeper in your experience of God.

As you end this chapter, take time to write down your answers to the following questions and then share those responses with your partner or group.

- Which of the Holy Spirit's special classes are you taking at this time, and which ones do you want to take in the future?

- Thinking about your life is a great way to determine how God might be calling you to take a special class. Are you going through some hard times? Are you enjoying some new opportunities to minister to others? Which Scripture passages are meaningful to you right now? (By the way, don't worry if you seem to repeat some of the lessons you learn. It seems to be part of the normal Christian life.)

Chapter Three:

Our Father's Multifaceted Ways

Anne Morrow Lindbergh, a noted writer and aviation pioneer and the widow of aviator and conservationist Charles A. Lindbergh, Jr., once remarked, "Good communication is as stimulating as black coffee, and just as hard to sleep after." How true that is! Have you ever come home from a date or a Bible study in which you've had an intense conversation and then tried to fall asleep? It's practically impossible.

As we read in this chapter, James Goll describes God's ability to keep you awake. When God wants to speak, it's like trying to fall asleep after a triple espresso! James writes:

God's life-giving word proceeds and continues to proceed. It is God's ever-proceeding word that gives us life! God has spoken; God is speaking; God will continue to guide His children (p. 38).

· Think about the different ways you experienced God speaking to you during the past week. Think about everything that happened. Do you remember a bit of a dream? Did a verse from the Bible jump off the page at you? Did you experience deep peace? Did your spirit say "amen" to one of the points in your pastor's sermon? Did a friend call to encourage you?

As a young Christian in the Jesus Movement, James Goll had a life-changing encounter when a man who had the gift of discernment challenged him by saying, "It's not that God has quit speaking. It's that He has just switched channels on His dial. God has not quit speaking to you. He has just turned the knob over to a different channel that you are not used to hearing Him on" (p. 39).

· Describe a time when you felt God stopped speaking to you because the usual ways you heard from God did not seem to be working,

In this chapter, you were given 20 verses (pp. 40-41) that describe the different tools God uses to build into

His children. Read each passage and then respond to the following questions.

- In what ways have you either experienced these tools or heard of others who have heard God's voice in these ways?

- If a friend asked you, "How does God speak?" what would you tell him?

Wake Up!

God woke James up in the middle of the night by using the telephone and then pointed him toward Jeremiah 33:3: "Call to Me, and I will answer you, and I will tell you great and mighty things, which you do not know."

God loves to get our attention. The Holy Spirit has been waking people for thousands of years. Samuel, who had a knack for hearing the voice of God, had a similar experience as a young child.

- As you read 1 Samuel 3, think of as many similarities between Samuel's experience and the one the author described by completing this sentence: *God spoke to Samuel and James in a similar way by . . .*

One way to prepare your mind to hear God's voice is to repeat Samuel's response, "Speak, for Your servant is listening" (v. 10). Next time you feel as if God is trying to tell you something, find a quiet place, repeat that phrase and listen. As you listen, remember this comment from Quin Sherrer:

God can speak to us through an "internal witness" or a "knowing" in our innermost being, a settling peace, a conviction that the decision we might normally fret over is the right one. He can also speak through circumstances ("closed and open doors") or a seemingly serendipitous meeting that brings us an opportunity (p. 43).

Opening the Box

In this chapter, the author highlights Psalm 29:3-9. Read that passage and then reflect on the following questions.

- "The voice of the LORD is over the waters, the God of glory thunders" (v. 3). Has God ever grabbed your attention in a dramatic way? How?

- "The voice of the LORD breaks the cedars, the LORD breaks in pieces the cedars of Lebanon" (v. 5). Have you ever felt like you were "too dense" for the Lord to reach? Did God break through? How?

- "He makes Lebanon skip like a calf, Sirion like a young wild ox" (v. 6). Have you ever needed to be refreshed by the Lord? Have you lost some of your zeal along the way? The intimacy of hearing His voice will make you skip once again.

- "The voice of the LORD hews out flames of fire" (v. 7). Has God ever purified you with His Word? Why do you think God did that?

139

LORD shakes the wilderness" (v. 8).
...nake our foundations to be sure that we
...r lives on a solid foundation. How has that
... to you?

As you finish this study, take time to worship God. Expect Him to draw near to you as you draw near to Him. Open your mind and heart to experience the many ways He might speak right now.

But be warned: Once you start communicating, you might be up most of the night!

Chapter Four:

Our Kingdom Birthright— Our Kingdom Walk

Take a moment to read the following Scripture passage out loud. After reading, jot down how the passage impacts the way you view your position in the kingdom of God.

> But you are a chosen race, a royal priesthood, a holy nation, a people for God's own possession, so that you may proclaim the excellencies of Him who has called you out of darkness into His marvelous light (1 Pet. 2:9).

· What are some of the rights and privileges of being part of God's kingdom?

> *As full citizens and members of this royal priesthood of the Lord, we have the right to request, at any time, a personal audience with the Master of the Universe* (p. 50).

· What thoughts come to your mind when you realize that you've been given direct access to the Creator of everything?

As we have learned over the past few chapters, we not only have the right to speak to God, but also God desires to speak to us. As His special possessions, God will give direction, guidance, correction and love. But even when we understand that God wants to speak, we sometimes hesitate to listen.

· Do you have any preconceived ideas that would stop you from continuing in the process of listening to God? If so, what are they?

James Goll describes the ability to hear God's voice as a "long-term learning process" (p. 51). He offers three warnings up front about the process of learning to hear the voice of God.

First, you must be willing to fail. Just as a baby needs to fall many times before she can walk, you too will fall. The author describes one of his first experiences trying to listen to God in a group setting. You can imagine his embarrassment when he said, "livers" instead of "rivers" to the amusement of the others in the room.

> *We all must learn lessons of humility, swallow some pride, seek the Lord for strength and wisdom and move on past mistakes. The important thing is to* keep moving on.

...ot unpardonable. We all have made
... make them in the future. We must learn
...stakes. We need to turn them over to our
...d let Him use them for His own glory (p. 53).

...e you ever had a time when you stepped out in faith only to discover you had made a mistake? What feelings did you have during and after that event?

One of the most well-known disciples in history began his walk with the risen Lord after a huge failure. On the night the Roman soldiers crucified Jesus, Peter followed behind to see what would happen. Three times Peter was asked if he knew Jesus and three times he denied it. Peter failed God miserably.

But God did not let Peter wallow in his mistakes. He called Peter to get up and keep moving.

Read John 21:1-19 and think about how Jesus invited Peter back into fellowship.

The second warning the author offers us is a reminder about the importance of learning to discern God's voice *one step at a time.* One misconception that many of us need to unlearn revolves around the perceived "absence of God."

Consider the story of a man who not only knew God's voice but also spoke for God in the face of great opposition. Elijah spent years hearing God and speaking for Him. He held the respect of kings (even though they wanted to kill him) and common people as one who knew the voice of God.

No one could have predicted that after one of his greatest successes in knowing the will of God, Elijah would be thrown into the depths of despair because he felt God had abandoned him. Read 1 Kings 19:1-18 and consider the following questions.

• What is significant about the ways God did *not* speak?

• How did Elijah respond when he finally heard God's voice?

• What do you think he learned from this experience?

As you develop your ability to hear God's voice, don't be surprised if you find that God has you finding new ways to listen.

The third warning the author offers is to emphasize that there are no shortcuts to learning to hear God's voice. Simply put, it's going to take time. We need to take time daily over a period of years. James Goll writes:

> *Our Western society does not teach us the art of listening. But the connection is obvious: If we want to hear, we must listen. I recommend speaking a little less and listening a whole lot more. Here's another hint: If we don't make time, He will help us to make time. He knows how to get our attention* (p. 55).

• What thoughts did you have as you read about James's experience of learning to listen for God's voice in the middle of the night?

• Are there things you love in your life that might become a hindrance to taking time to listen for God's voice?

As you pray this week, try taking time to sit quietly and simply listen. Begin to train your ear to "hear the slightest whisper of God." You'll have to stop speaking in order to listen. As an experiment, spend half your prayer time this week in silence and journal what you hear God speaking.

Chapter Five:

Our Road Map

Have you ever had the experience of knowing that you had to be at a certain place at a certain time and you had only a vague idea as to how to get there? But instead of asking for directions, you just jumped into your car hoping everything would work out. What happened?

If you are like most people, sometimes it works out and sometimes it doesn't. You drive around frantically, saying to yourself, *I know it's around here somewhere! I wish I had written down the directions before I left.*

Nobody likes to be lost. For many, the idea of listening to God's voice and understanding His will is a lot like trying to get somewhere without a map. We only have a vague idea how to get there.

Fortunately, God has given us a complete map. James Goll writes:

> God has not left us on our own, mapless or helpless, to try to figure out how to get to His destinations. He has given us our personal Tutor, the Holy Spirit, to guide us

*into all truth. He has also given us His road map of life,
the Word of God* (pp. 61-62).

· Psalm 119:105 reads, "Your word is a lamp to my feet
and a light to my path." What thoughts come to your
mind when you consider that God's Word is a light as
you move toward Him?

· Describe a time when you needed guidance and the
Scriptures gave you that direction.

Get Out the Map

In this chapter, the author makes a passionate appeal for
those who want to discern God's voice to become students of God's road map, the Bible. He writes:

> *To complete our journey with the Lord, we must study,
> read and meditate on the written Word of God. As we
> read it and chew on it, His Word will begin to dwell
> richly in our heart and mind* (p. 62).

The author describes his relationship with an old
friend: his favorite Bible. While he has many different
Bibles, this particular Bible had become a close companion for over 20 years. It was filled with sermon notes, his
kid's scribblings (red ink through 1 Peter!) and a variety
of other marks that showed it had been well loved.

· How about you? What Bible do you use and write down
notes in?

If you do not have a Bible that has become your personal guide, consider finding one that you would like to use over the years. The first step to following a map is to get one! The next step is allowing the Word of God to become a part of who you are.

Read the Map

Colossians 3:16 says, "Let the word of Christ dwell in you richly as you teach and admonish one another with all wisdom, and as you sing psalms, hymns and spiritual songs with gratitude in your hearts to God."

• As a group or with a friend, use your imagination to create a list of four things you can do each day to help you let the Word of Christ dwell richly in you.

The author describes the Word of God dwelling in your heart by using the image of his mother storing up food for the winter during the summer. He writes:

> Just as my mother stored fruit, vegetables and produce to be used, eaten and enjoyed at a later date, so too we store up the written Word of God (logos *in Greek*) so that it later can be "eaten" as a life-producing spoken word (rhema *in Greek*) (pp. 64-65).

• In your own words, describe the difference between the *logos* of God and the *rhema* of God.

Follow the Directions

When children learn to read, often they read a couple of pages with great enthusiasm, concentrating on each and every word. As they finish their assignment, the teacher asks, "Now, what was the story about?" and the students' smile quickly turns to a blank stare. They have no idea. They read but had no understanding.

In this chapter you are invited to slow down and understand the words of Scripture through meditation. James Goll writes:

> *We can read the Word. We can pray based on the words we read. But the approach to the Scriptures that will best help us to turn the logos into rhema is the spiritual discipline of meditating on the Word of Life* (pp. 67-68).

· When you hear the word "meditate," what images come to your mind?

Let's put this into practice. First, read the following passage:

> Let the word of Christ dwell in you richly as you teach and admonish one another with all wisdom, and as you sing psalms, hymns and spiritual songs with gratitude in your heart to God (Col. 3:16).

Now, follow these steps: (1) Ask the Holy Spirit to speak to you through this exercise. (2) Sit quietly for a moment and then read the passage slowly, listening for words or phrases that God might be highlighting. (3) Sit quietly and listen for God's voice. (4) Read the passage again slowly. (5) Ask God to give you an image or a word from this passage.

Share with a friend or your group what you heard from God's Word.

Just as the people of Israel were called to collect manna daily, we too need to go to the Word of God daily and let it dwell richly in us. Consider what would happen in your life if each day, every day, you took 15 minutes to meditate on God's Word.

• Do you take time every day to gather manna from the Scriptures? What can you do to grow in this area?

Make a commitment this week to spend daily time in God's Word.

Chapter Six:

Our Practical Tools

As we studied in the last chapter, knowing the Word of God and then speaking it into action generates the possibility of discerning God's voice. As you spent time in God's Word, did you experience a word of revelation from God?

Ten Effective Tools for Hearing

This chapter presents 10 tools that will assist you in the art of hearing and following the voice of God. As you investigate how these tools apply to your walk with God, decide which tool would be most important for you to put into practice over the next few weeks.

1. Don't Make It Complicated!
The author offers three simple steps to prepare your mind and spirit to communicate with God.

Step One: Submit to His Lordship. Read Proverbs 3:5-7. Think about a time when your pre-formed thoughts and ideas prevented you from being able to hear God's direction in your life. Write a simple prayer of submission that will help you give your thoughts and ideas over to God.

Step Two: Resist the enemy. Read James 4:7. Think about some typical techniques the devil might use to prevent you from hearing God's voice. Develop a strategy to resist these attacks.

Step Three: Ask a question and expect God's answer. Read Colossians 1:9. Rarely does God answer like the Instant Messenger on your computer. James Goll writes:

> *We should not expect to get an answer to pop right up ("You've got mail!"); rather, we should wait expectantly, believing that as we have submitted to God and resisted the enemy, we will be "filled with the knowledge of His will in all spiritual wisdom and understanding"* (p. 75).

- Do you have trouble waiting patiently on God? What are some ways that you can develop an attitude of patient expectation?

2. Allow God to Speak as He Chooses

As we discovered in chapter three, God speaks in a variety of ways. Review the 20 passages of Scripture you studied in that chapter.

- With a friend, discuss the most surprising way you've heard from God. How does God usually speak to you or people you know?

3. Confess Any Known Sins

Make a commitment to begin your prayer and study time confessing your sins and seeking God's forgiveness.

- Have you made confession of sin a regular part of your time with the Lord? Begin today.

4. Obey the Last Thing God Said

This tool relates closely to the confession of sin. When God speaks, He expects you to act. It's a question of obedience.

- If you had a son or daughter who continually asked you for advice or counsel but never took your words seriously, how long would it take before you simply stopped giving advice?

- Read 2 Kings 6:4-7. Have you been keeping your axe sharp?

You can start right now. Tell someone how you sensed God speaking to you in the past and what you plan to do in response. If you have deliberately disobeyed, confess your sin to your friend and to God. Ask your friend to keep you accountable to follow through on your commitment.

5. Get Your Own Leading

Often young Christians become co-dependent on others for spiritual guidance. Because they don't trust their ability to hear God, they seek confirmation from others.

> *We need to become secure in our own identity in Christ. We must realize that we are sons and daughters of the Creator of the universe and that He wants to relate to us in our own right* (p. 78).

· In the past, have you trusted other people to the detriment of hearing God's voice on your own? If so, how? If not, what has helped you not to depend too heavily on others?

6. Don't Talk About Your Word Too Soon

Read the story of Joseph and his brothers as recorded in Genesis 37:2-11.

· What response did Joseph receive from his family when he related his visions?

· Review the four traps on pages 79-80. Into which of these traps do you think Joseph fell? Of the four traps, to which do you think you are most vulnerable?

7. Know That God Will Confirm What He's Telling You

God will give us our own stuff—there is plenty to go around, but we can depend on the fact that God does use others to confirm His word. It's part of His safety net of protection (2 Cor. 13:1: "Every fact is to be confirmed by the testimony of two or three witnesses") (p. 80).

Make a list of the people whom you trust to confirm the words God is speaking to you. Pray for those who have authority over you that they will be guided by the Holy Spirit.

8. Beware of Counterfeits

Have you or someone you know ever experienced counterfeit guidance through psychics, the New Age movement or other means? How did that experience differ from what you know about hearing God's voice?

If you have experienced that type of guidance, confess it to God and ask Him to remove any foothold that the devil might have in your life.

9. Practice Hearing God's Voice

In this section, the author relates the story of not recognizing his sister's voice on the telephone.

- Have you ever had a time when God spoke to you but you weren't really sure who was speaking?

- Over the past few weeks of listening for God's voice, do you feel like you are getting to know His voice better?

- What has been satisfying and what has been frustrating about your experience?

10. Cultivate an Intimate Relationship
Read John 10:1-7.

- Are you cultivating your relationship with the Good Shepherd? He longs to spend time with you and for you to spend time with Him.

- As you have studied these tools, which of the tools do you need most to learn how to use?

- Which of these tools do you find the easiest to use? Why is this the case?

Chapter Seven:

Our Brothers, Our Sisters

- Which of these statements is true?

    A. The greatest assets to revealing God's character and voice in your community are Christians who worship in your city/town.

    B. The greatest liability to revealing God's character and voice in your community are Christians who worship in your city/town.

- Are the Christians who you know an asset or liability to others' ability to see and hear God?

In God's infinite wisdom, His primary vehicle of communication is through people. In fact, He became a person for just that reason. God demonstrated His love in the person of Jesus of Nazareth. And how did Jesus reveal God's love and will? He revealed God's love through His actions and words. We are to do the same.

As our author writes:

We are His children, and we are supposed to look, act and talk like Him as His representatives on Earth. But is the world able to see the Father's love in us? Moreover, can we see and hear our Papa God in and through our brothers and sisters? (pp. 86-87).

Checking for Earplugs

After reading the Scripture passage below, ask God to reveal to you the parts of the Body of Christ and people in your life you would never expect Him to use.

If the foot says, "Because I am not a hand, I am not a part of the body," it is not for this reason any the less a part of the body. And if the ear says, "Because I am not an eye, I am not a part of the body," it is not for this reason any the less a part of the body. If the whole body were an eye, where would the hearing be? If the whole were hearing, where would the sense of smell be? But now God has placed the members, each one of them, in the body, just as He desired (1 Cor. 12:15-18).

· Complete the following prayers of confession:

— Lord, the parts of Your Body I would not expect You to speak through are . . .

—

— Lord, the people I would never expect You to speak through are . . .

From the two lists you've created, pray that God will use someone you've listed to speak directly to you.

· Reflect on the following words from this chapter and then think about a time when someone gave you a word from God, but you did not listen because of your prejudice:

We set our own strict little boundaries about how and through whom God can speak to us. We make a select list. Then, wham, somebody messes with our list. We don't know what hit us, so we rebuke the devil. Later on, after we've become more humble, we learn it was God (p. 88).

James Goll describes two different experiences when God taught him that He speaks through unexpected people: with his wife, Michal Ann, and during the Jesus Movement in America in the 1970s. He speculates whether God takes joy in surprising us by the people He chooses.

Do you think God enjoys watching our shock at the ways He chooses to speak?

Go Wash in the River

Read 2 Kings 5:1-27 and consider the following questions.

- Make a list of all the people who had an influence in the healing of Naaman.

- Consider all the possible reasons why Naaman was at first offended by the simple request to wash in a river. Have you had an experience similar to Naaman's in which "God offends the mind to reveal the heart"?

- What lessons do you learn about listening to God's voice from this story?

Like Naaman, all of us have barriers in our ability to hear God's voice. The author describes two types of people: HTR (hard to receive) and ETR (easy to receive). Consider his description of the best way to break down barriers for those of us who are HTRs:

> *My advice to HTRs: Spend lots of time simply worshiping God. Worship has been a major key the Master has used to transform many hearts. Giant oak trees of stubbornness and fear fall before the transforming love of our Father* (p. 92).

- Why do you think worship is such an effective tool for breaking down barriers to hearing God's voice?

- Of the barriers listed below, consider which ones get in the way of your own ability to hear God's voice.

    ___ Lack of faith
    ___ Lack of a strong commitment to Jesus as Lord
    ___ The presence of sin
    ___ Ignorance of the Scripture
    ___ Lack of quality teaching
    ___ Fear of man and rejection
    ___ Fear of being deceived
    ___ Guilty feelings
    ___ Hurts from the past

As you reflect on the obstacles God wants to break down in your life, consider James Goll's powerful words:

We can overcome any and all of the barriers that remain between us and God. There is healing for any ailment that has ever existed. The cure is as old as the universe itself. It is the love of God. Love heals (p. 93).

Psalm 103 expresses God's great love for you and can serve as a way for you to worship Him. Experiencing the love of God will help you to discern His voice.

Take time to read Psalm 103 each day throughout the coming week. Read it slowly and allow it to seep into your heart as a time of worship and a time of receiving God's love. As you read, write down your thoughts and feelings about God and His love for you.

Receiving Love Through the Body

In this chapter, the author describes his experience with cancer and how the love of other Christians became a tangible example of God's love to him and his family. As He received God's love through prayers and acts of kindness, the powers of darkness were defeated.

- Have you ever had a time when believers in your life demonstrated the power and love of God to you? If you have not personally, has someone you know had this experience? What did that experience teach you about the love of God?

    Consider:

    If we want to see barriers in our heart and soul dissolve, we must ask the Holy Spirit to help us receive the gift of love that proceeds from our brothers and sisters. In a circular fashion, what goes around will come around. We will become a channel of God's love for them too (p. 94).

    Ask God to break down any barriers that get in the way of you hearing His voice through others. Pray for your church and the community of believers in your town that you might be a powerful witness for Christ in your region.

Chapter Eight:

Our Need to Discern

Over the past seven studies, you've had the opportunity to hear and experience the voice of God. Hopefully, you've experienced God's comfort, His challenge and His call as His will has been revealed.

In chapter eight, James Goll gives a warning to those who desire to grow in spirit-to-Spirit communication: *God is not the only voice that wants to lead you.* As you have sought spiritual revelation, have you felt that you might be hearing God's voice but you weren't sure?

Read how Jesus described the reality of other voices in John 10:1-6, and then answer the following questions:

· Who do you think Jesus was talking about when He described someone who climbs in the sheep pen as a thief and a robber?

· Why would someone want to steal the sheep?

· How do sheep come to know the Shepherd's voice and why do they run away from a stranger's voice?

· Why is it important to be able to discern the voice of God from other voices?

Consider this wisdom from C. Peter Wagner:

The gift of discerning of spirits is the special ability that God gives to certain members of the Body of Christ to know with assurance whether certain behavior purported to be God is in reality divine, human or satanic (p. 98).

· Think of a few examples from your experience in the Body of Christ of behaviors that would be considered divine, human or satanic.

Are you able to tell the difference between the different voices that vie for your attention? A wolf will do whatever it can to get to the sheep—even put on sheep's clothing—but as the author writes:

> *The wolf may look like a sheep, but he still smells like a wolf. In Scripture, discernment is like a sense of smell, acting independently of the natural eyesight* (p. 99).

The first Christians were the first to experience how the Holy Spirit reveals which voices come from God and which voices are "wolves in sheep's clothing." After reading these three accounts from the book of Acts, contemplate what tipped the apostles off that they were dealing with spiritual voices *not* inspired by the Holy Spirit: Acts 16:16-18; 13:6-12; 8:20-24.

Understanding Revelation

Sometimes God speaks as we expect. We hear His quiet voice as we pray or through words of comfort from a pastor or friend. Sometimes, however, God speaks in extraordinary ways. Ways that might make us feel as if we are going crazy! Consider the following examples from Scripture of how God revealed Himself to these faithful saints. After you read each account, think about how people in your church would react if these prophets gave their testimonies: Isaiah 6:1-10; Ezekiel 37; Acts 9:1-19.

James Goll writes:

> *Most of us in the Western world, if confronted with such events, would tend to chalk them up to psychological dis-*

*turbances or the devil. Entire segments of the Body of
Christ have written off hearing from the Lord because of
fears about being led astray* (p. 100).

· Why do you think people in the Western world often
have a hard time experiencing supernatural encounters
with God?

The author describes three sources of spiritual communication: the Holy Spirit, the human soul and evil spirits. In order to grow your ability to hear God's voice, you
need to be able to discern between these three types of
spiritual communication.

· Describe a time when you've experienced the Holy Spirit's
voice and what happened as a result.

· Have you ever thought you heard God but then discovered it was really your own thought? What happened?

· List some ways that evil spirits may lead people astray in
your church or community.

Review the nine scriptural tests (pp. 103-105). In your
own words, how would you explain each test to someone
who wanted to develop discernment?

1. Does the revelation edify, exhort or console?

2. Is it in agreement with God's Word?

3. Does it exalt Jesus Christ?

4. Does it have good fruit?

5. If it predicts a future event, does it come to pass?

6. Does the revelatory turn people toward God or away from Him?

7. Does it produce liberty or bondage?

8. Does it produce life or death?

9. Does the Holy Spirit bear witness that it is true?

- Read Acts 10, the story of Peter and Cornelius. Apply the nine scriptural tests to Peter's vision. Does his experience pass the tests?

Ask for Wisdom and Discernment

Wisdom (which helps us know what to do next) goes hand in hand with discernment (which helps us know the source of what we observe). We need both in order to experience the full and abundant life God desires for us.

As a group or with a friend, discuss the following questions and then take time to pray for each other to increase in wisdom and discernment.

- Are you stronger in one of these qualities than the other?

- Are you lacking in one or both of them?

- Do you have trusted friends who can help you compensate for your relative weakness by giving wise counsel or by confirming your own discernment?

Chapter Nine:

Our Geiger Counter of Guidance

You do not have to walk through life alone, bored or lost. You have a Guide who will take you on a God-sized adventure! When others suffer through the day-to-day grind, your Personal Tutor will teach you new things each day and lead you to places (both spiritual and physical) you've only read about in books. You literally can experience what you've read about in Scripture.

Read the following Scripture passage out loud at least twice, and then write down any thoughts and images that come to your mind:

> Although the Lord has given you bread of privation and water of oppression, He, your Teacher will no longer hide Himself, but your eyes will behold your Teacher. Your ears will hear a word behind you, "This is the way, walk in it," whenever you turn to the right or to the left (Isa. 30:20-21).

· What images and thoughts did you receive through this passage?

The author uses the metaphor of a Geiger counter to describe God's guidance. He writes:

I have often thought this is a lot like our approach to hearing God's voice. Our spirit is like the Geiger counter that tells us whether we are closer or farther away. It helps us put all the pieces together. We learn to pay attention to an inner witness (p. 108).

- Describe a time when the Holy Spirit created an outburst in you like the clicking of a Geiger counter.

Many Christians operate like a carpenter who owns a tool box full of tools but only uses his hammer. While a hammer works well for driving a nail into a piece of wood, it's almost useless as a level. The carpenter needs to open the toolbox and become familiar with all his available tools.

In the same way, to become mature and equipped to discern God's voice, we need to be familiar with the many tools available. In this chapter, the author describes 10 different principles to "help you hear God's voice, determine His guidance and, most of all, grow closer to God Himself" (p. 108). Review each of these principles and answer the questions below.

1. The Will of God Is Made Known in the Word of God

- How well do you know God's Word (objective logos)?

- Describe a time when your feelings were leading you to do something that was contrary to God's Word, yet you felt God was telling you to do it.

2. The Will of God Is Confirmed Through Circumstances

- Give an example of a time when circumstances helped you know God's will.

- Give an example of a time when circumstances seemed to point one way but God told you something different.

3. The Holy Spirit Speaks from Where He Dwells
Read John 16:13 and consider that the Holy Spirit dwells within you and gives you guidance. What are some thoughts and feelings you have about this reality?

4. Divine Guidance Comes from Meeting God's Conditions
Read Isaiah 58 and make a list of the various requirements that God has given for us to more effectively understand His will.

5. Peace of God Accompanies True Guidance
Read Philippians 4:6-7 and think about what aspects of prayer you can practice to know God's will and experience His peace.

6. Much Guidance from God Comes Unnoticed
With informed hindsight, reflect on a circumstance in your life that illustrates this principle. What guidance has come that you acknowledge now but that you did not recognize at the moment?

7. Divine Guidance Does Not Mean We Know All the Details

- Reflecting on the author's metaphor of a child watching a parade, think of a word picture that describes how you feel about your ability to hear and understand God's guidance in your life.

• Are you someone who needs to know everything, or are you comfortable living with ambiguity, knowing that God is in control?

8. The Process of Guidance Is Not Always Pleasant
Read Isaiah 55:8-9 and think about a time when God's thoughts were very different than your thoughts. How did that situation work out?

9. Hearing God Speak Should Prompt Us to Action
What was the last thing God asked you to do? Have you completed it? Why or why not? Make a commitment to follow through on God's guidance this week.

10. Guidance Is a Skill to Be Learned Over a Lifetime
Take a moment to imagine what you hope your Christian life will look like in 20 years. Will you have walked with God closely from now until then? What can you do today to make sure that happens?

Choose 1 of these 10 principles of divine guidance and tell somebody how it has worked for you. If you don't have someone to tell, write down your thoughts about how you relied on the principle.

Chapter Ten:
Our Journey's End

Have you ever attended a graduation ceremony? After working hard for years, the graduates have finally completed their journey. Tears flow as they realize that part of their lives is over. And yet, life is not over—it is just beginning! A grand adventure awaits as they put into practice everything they've learned.

You've come to the end of your School of the Spirit. Like graduation, however, this is not an end but instead the beginning of the exciting adventure of following God's voice.

Reflect on these words the apostle Paul wrote after following Christ for years:

> Not that I have already obtained it or have already become perfect, but I press on so that I may lay hold of that for which also I was laid hold of by Christ Jesus. Brethren, I do not regard myself as having laid hold of it yet; but one thing I do: forgetting what lies behind and reaching forward to what lies ahead, I press on toward the goal for the prize of the upward call of God in Christ Jesus (Phil. 3:12-14).

· Consider three words that describe the Christian life according to these verses.

James Goll writes:

> *Learning from the lessons of believers who have gone before us, we realize that all progress in the Christian life comes by faith. We turn to our road map over and over again. We lean our ear in His direction to receive encouragement for today. Yes, it may be an arduous path, but it is indeed an adventure* (p. 118).

• What excites you about the adventure of following God? What fears do you have?

Has God Said?

Satan wants to ruin God's adventure in your life. Fortunately for us, his tactics have been well recorded. The author reminds us that Satan first caused Eve to question her understanding of God's voice and then he manipulated her into disobeying God's commands.

Scripture also records how Jesus stood firm when Satan used the same tactics against Him. Compare these two encounters and answer the following questions:

• Read Genesis 3:1-7 and Matthew 4:1-11. What tactics did Satan use against Eve and Jesus?

• How did Satan manipulate Eve? How did Jesus stand firm when He was tempted?

• What pitfalls can you avoid as you learn from Eve's mistakes? What principles can you learn from Jesus' encounter with Satan?

The early Christians heard the same stories. They knew that like a general hell-bent on destroying his enemy, Satan would not give up, even after his defeat by Jesus. After the resurrection, he turned his eyes on the followers of Christ. But the early Christians were taught techniques to confront the enemy. Read Ephesians 6:10-18 and think about how the early Christians took their stand against the forces of evil.

Like a great coach, God not only shows us how to stand against Satan, but He also gives us tests—opportunities—to strengthen our faith. When you say "Yes!" to following the Spirit's adventure, God will lead you to places that will prove your character to the world.

Consider these words from the author:

> *Often, when we receive an exciting revelation from God, He uses the revelation itself to test us and purify us so that our character will be able to convey the word to others* (p. 120).

• In what ways has God already begun the refining process in your life?

• What has been the biggest faith challenge you've faced so far?

Our author mentions four men who were tested by God over a period of years. Abraham, Joseph, Moses and David were far from perfect. They had the same fears, doubts and lack of trust we have, yet God used them to do great things. They also had something else we have: the ability to hear God's voice and say, "Yes, I will follow."

Read the following passages and consider God's refining work in each person.

• Genesis 22 (Abraham)
• Genesis 45 (Joseph)
• Exodus 32 (Moses)
• 2 Samuel 15 (David)

- Would you be willing to follow God as they followed Him?

  James Goll writes:

  Should we be exceptions to this pattern? If we can hear God's voice and have been called to even a small task in building His kingdom, let's rejoice that we have been found worthy to be called God's children and to be tested on the very promises He gives to us (p. 122).

- How does 1 Corinthians 10:13 speak to any fears you might have?

  As you consider your walk with Christ, reflect on these questions:

  How many times have I allowed God's word to slip away because I thought the testings were simply evidence that I had heard it wrong? How many times did I lose out when the little voice said, Did God *really* say that? (p. 123).

Your Ministry to the Nations (or Neighborhood)

The author describes a powerful experience with the Holy Spirit when he received his first vision of God's plan for his life. The Holy Spirit not only showed God's will, but the Personal Tutor also helped him to live it out. As he mentions, following God can come at a great cost. But as the author gave up his own will for his life, God gave him a life of unimaginable adventure and fulfillment.

As you come to the end of this study, meditate on the following words of Jesus:

> If anyone wishes to come after Me, he must deny himself, and take up his cross and follow Me. For whoever wishes to save his life will lose it; but whoever loses his life for My sake will find it (Matt. 16:24-25).

Are you willing to follow God no matter where He leads and to discover His perfect will for your life?

> *Do you hear Him speaking to you now? He's waiting to have a moment just with you. Lean your head a bit and you will hear more than words. You will hear the sound of love beating in His heart. He is your journey's end. Knowing God is what hearing God is ultimately all about!* (p. 126).

As you finish this study, thank God for what you have learned and make a commitment to continue in your quest to know Him and hear His voice.

Endnotes

Chapter One: Our Need to Hear God

1. Mark Virkler, quoted in Leonard LeSourd, ed., *Touching the Heart of God* (Old Tappan, NJ: Chosen Books, 1990), p. 59.
2. Dutch Sheets, quoted in Quin Sherrer, *Listen, God Is Speaking to You* (Ann Arbor, MI: Vine Books, 1999), p. 9.
3. James W. Goll, *The Coming Prophetic Revolution* (Grand Rapids, MI: Chosen Books, 2001), p. 28.
4. Fuchsia Pickett, *Receiving Divine Revelation* (Lake Mary, FL: Creation House, 1977), p. 15.

Chapter Two: Our Personal Tutor

1. Quin Sherrer and Ruthanne Garlock, *The Beginner's Guide to Receiving the Holy Spirit* (Ann Arbor, MI: Vine Books, 2002), p. 45.
2. David Wilkerson, "What It Means to Walk in the Spirit," *Times Square Church Pulpit Series* (August 15, 1994), p. 4.
3. *Merriam-Webster's Collegiate Dictionary, 10th edition*, s.v. "tutor."

Chapter Three: Our Father's Multifaceted Ways

1. James W. Goll, *The Coming Prophetic Revolution* (Grand Rapids, MI: Chosen Books, 2001), p. 125.
2. Quin Sherrer, *Listen, God Is Speaking to You* (Ann Arbor, MI: Vine Books, 1999), p. 26.
3. Ibid., pp. 25-26.

Chapter Four: Our Kingdom Birthright—Our Kingdom Walk

1. Jack Deere, *Surprised by the Power of the Spirit* (Grand Rapids, MI: Zondervan Publishing House, 1993), p. 212.
2. James W. Goll, *The Coming Prophetic Revolution* (Grand Rapids, MI: Chosen Books, 2001), pp. 19-20.
3. Michael Brown, *Revolution! The Call to Holy War* (Ventura, CA: Renew, 2000), pp. 57-58.
4. Sam Storms, *The Beginner's Guide to Spiritual Gifts* (Ann Arbor, MI: Vine Books, 2002), pp. 17-18.

Chapter Five: Our Road Map

1. *Vine's Expository Dictionary of the New Testament* (Old Tappan, NJ: Fleming H. Revel Company, 1966), p. 230.
2. James W. Goll, *Wasted on Jesus* (Shippensburg, PA: Destiny Image, 2000), pp. 97-98.
3. Peter Toon, *Meditating as a Christian* (London: HarperCollins, 1991), p. 61.
4. Richard Foster, *Prayer: Finding the Heart's True Home* (San Francisco: HarperSanFrancisco, 1992), p. 146.

Chapter Six: Our Practical Tools

1. The content of this chapter has been greatly inspired by, though not directly quoted from, the outstanding book *Is That Really You, God?* by Loren Cunningham. Loren Cunningham is the founder of Youth With A Mission. I would highly recommend this book to anyone desiring to learn more about hearing and discerning the voice of God. Used by permission.

Chapter Seven: Our Brothers, Our Sisters

1. James Goll and Michal Ann Goll, *Encounters with a Supernatural God* (Shippensburg, PA: Destiny Image, 1998), p. 2.
2. Ibid., p. 13.
3. James W. Goll, *Prophetic Foundations* (Franklin, TN: Ministry to the Nations, 2000), p. 35.
4. James W. Goll, *The Coming Prophetic Revolution* (Grand Rapids, MI: Chosen Books, 2001), p. 28.

Chapter Eight: Our Need to Discern

1. James W. Goll, *Releasing Spiritual Gifts* (Franklin, TN: Ministry to the Nations, 2000), p. 30.
2. Sam Storms, *The Beginner's Guide to Spiritual Gifts* (Ann Arbor, MI: Vine Books, 2002), pp. 103-104.
3. James Goll and Michal Ann Goll, *Encounters with a Supernatural God* (Shippensburg, PA: Destiny Image, 1998), pp. 151-154. Paraphrased and used by permission.

Chapter Ten: Our Journey's End

1. Maltbie D. Babcock, "This Is My Father's World," words 1901, public domain.

Recommended Reading

Books by James W. Goll

The Coming Prophetic Revolution (Chosen Books, 2001)

Experiencing Dreams and Visions (Ministry to the Nations, 2000)

Prophetic Foundations (Ministry to the Nations, 2000)

Releasing Spiritual Gifts (Ministry to the Nations, 2000)

Books by Others

Cunningham, Loren. *Is That Really You, Lord?*
Seattle, WA: YWAM Publishing, 1984.

Deere, Jack. *Surprised by the Voice of God.*
Grand Rapids, MI: Zondervan Publishing House, 1993.

Jacobs, Cindy. *The Voice of God.*
Ventura, CA: Regal Books, 2000.

Prince, Derek. *How to Judge Prophecy.*
Charlotte, NC: Derek Prince Publications, 1971.

Sherrer, Quin. *Listen, God Is Speaking to You.*
Ann Arbor, MI: Vine Books, 1999.

Virkler, Mark. *Communion with God.*
Shippensburg, PA: Destiny Image, 1990.

Dr. James W. Goll and his wife, Michal Ann, are the co-founders of Encounters Network (formerly Ministry to the Nations) in Franklin, Tennessee. James is the Director of Prayer Storm, a member of the Harvest International Ministries Apostolic Team, an instructor in the Wagner Leadership Institute and serves on numerous national and international councils. He is also a contributing writer for *Kairos* magazine.

Study guides, CDs, DVDs and books by James and Michal Ann Goll are available through the Resource Center of Encounters Network. Information about conferences, missions outreaches, training opportunities and email communiqués can be found on the EN website.

For more information:

Encounters Network
P.O. Box 1653
Franklin, TN 37065
Phone: 1-877-200-1604
Website: www.jamesgoll.com
Email: admin@encountersnetwork.com

More Great Resources from Regal

The Voice of God
How God Speaks Personally and
Corporately to His Children Today
Cindy Jacobs
ISBN 978.08307.36386

Dreams and Visions
Understanding Your Dreams and How God
Can Use Them to Speak to You Today
Jane Hamon
ISBN 978.08307.25694

Yes, Lord!
Harald Bredesen & Pat King
ISBN 978.08307.45357

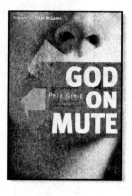

God on Mute
Engaging the Silence of Unanswered Prayer
Pete Greig
ISBN 978.08307.43247

Available at Bookstores Everywhere!
Visit **www.regalbooks.com** to join **Regal's FREE e-newsletter.**
You'll get useful **excerpts from our newest releases** and **special
access to online chats with your favorite authors.** Sign up today!

Regal
God's Word for Your World™
www.regalbooks.com